THE KINGFISHER
ENCYCLOPEDIA OF
LIFE

Copyright © Kingfisher 2012
Published in the United States by Kingfisher,
175 Fifth Ave., New York, NY 10010
Kingfisher is an imprint of Macmillan Children's Books, London.

Distributed in the U.S. and Canada by Macmillan, 175 Fifth Ave.,
New York, NY 10010

Library of Congress Cataloging-in-Publication data has been
applied for.

ISBN: 978-0-7534-7193-7

Kingfisher books are available for special promotions and
premiums. For details contact: Special Markets Department,
Macmillan, 175 Fifth Ave., New York, NY 10010.

For more information, please visit www.kingfisherbooks.com

Printed in China
9 8 7 6 5 4 3 2 1
1TR/0614/WKT/UG/128MA

Conceived and produced for Kingfisher by Heritage Editorial
Editorial Direction Andrew Heritage, Ailsa C. Heritage
Design Philippa Baile at Oil Often (www.oiloften.co.uk)
Illustrations Andy Crisp (www.andycrisp.co.uk)

Note to readers: the website addresses listed in this book
are correct at the time of going to print. However, due to the
ever-changing nature of the Internet, website addresses and
content can change. The publisher cannot be held responsible
for changes in website addresses or content or for information
obtained through a third party. We strongly advise that Internet
searches be supervised by an adult.

THE KINGFISHER
ENCYCLOPEDIA OF
LIFE

LIFE SPANS IN MINUTES, MONTHS, MILLENNIA

Dr. Graham L. Banes

KINGFISHER
NEW YORK

CONT

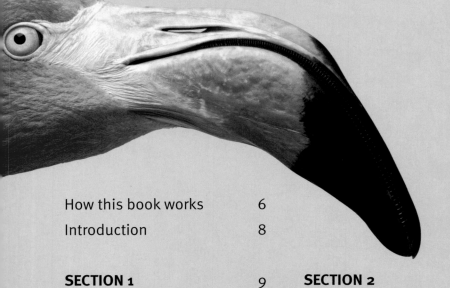

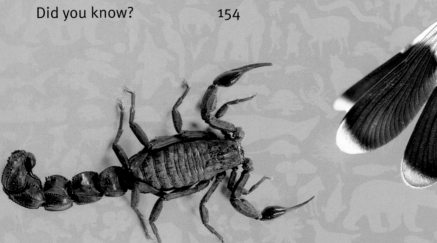

HOW THIS BOOK WORKS

The Kingfisher Encyclopedia of Life has been designed to provide readers with an imaginative introduction to the natural world and to the huge array of species that inhabit it. The information is organized according to the average life span or life cycle of each species.

The encyclopedia is divided into five main sections, which include three different types of double-page spreads. The various features of each spread are explained here.

Throughout the book, the species are organized into four separate groups. Each group is color-coded.

Microorganisms Species that are often too small to be seen with the naked eye.

Plants and fungi Plants, including their flowers, and fungi such as mushrooms and molds.

Invertebrates Animals with no backbone or spinal column.

Vertebrates Animals with a backbone or spinal column.

17 years **Circles** are used to indicate life cycles, for species that go through a number of developmental stages.

15 years **Squares** are used to indicate life spans. They denote species that normally live through just one developmental stage, such as humans (see page 116). They are also used when referring to the length of a specific developmental stage, such as the adult stage of butterflies (see page 17).

Species spreads look at a single species or families of similar species in detail.

The color band indicates the section of the book

General introduction to the species shown on the spread

Timescale of the spread

Silhouettes indicate the range of species shown on the spread

The arrow on the timeline shows the position of the spread in the overall timescale of the book

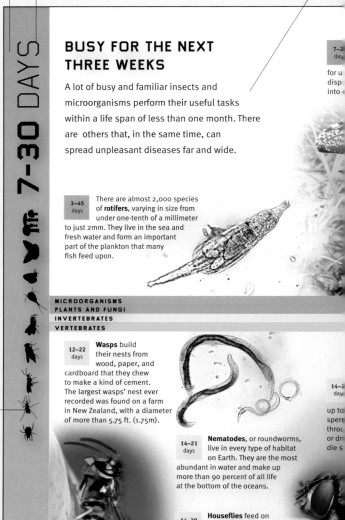

7-30 DAYS

BUSY FOR THE NEXT THREE WEEKS

A lot of busy and familiar insects and microorganisms perform their useful tasks within a life span of less than one month. There are others that, in the same time, can spread unpleasant diseases far and wide.

3–45 days There are almost 2,000 species of **rotifers**, varying in size from under one-tenth of a millimeter to just 2mm. They live in the sea and fresh water and form an important part of the plankton that many fish feed upon.

MICROORGANISMS
PLANTS AND FUNGI
INVERTEBRATES
VERTEBRATES

12–22 days **Wasps** build their nests from wood, paper, and cardboard that they chew to make a kind of cement. The largest wasps' nest ever recorded was found on a farm in New Zealand, with a diameter of more than 5.75 ft. (1.75m).

14–21 days **Nematodes,** or roundworms, live in every type of habitat on Earth. They are the most abundant in water and make up more than 90 percent of all life at the bottom of the oceans.

14–30 days **Houseflies** feed on rotting flesh and feces (poop). They spit saliva onto their food to liquefy it, then suck it up using an extendable mouth called a proboscis.

16

| I MONTH | I YEAR | 2 YEARS | 5 YEARS | IO YEARS | 20 YE |

50-75 YEARS

PARROTS

Parrots live mostly in tropical regions and use their large, curved beaks to crack open seeds and nuts. They can learn human words and phrases, imitate sounds, use tools, and solve complex problems. Their bright colors and intelligence have made parrots popular as pets, but many pet parrots are taken from the wild. This has caused wild populations to decline and threatens parrot species with extinction.

104

Squares indicate life span

Numbers show average life span or life cycle

! box provides an astonishing fact about one of the species on the spread

Circles indicate life cycle

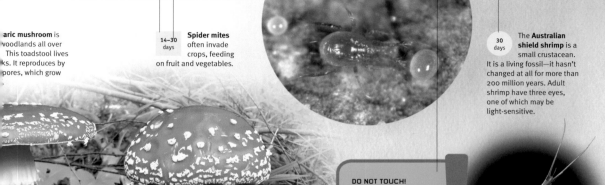

...aric mushroom is ...woodlands all over ... This toadstool lives ...ks. It reproduces by ...pores, which grow

14–30 days — **Spider mites** often invade crops, feeding on fruit and vegetables.

30 days — The **Australian shield shrimp** is a small crustacean. It is a living fossil—it hasn't changed at all for more than 200 million years. Adult shrimp have three eyes, one of which may be light-sensitive.

DO NOT TOUCH!
Although it is very pretty, the fly agaric mushroom is highly dangerous to eat and should never be touched.

Life span spreads present a range of species that share a similar life span or life cycle for one or all of the stages of their lives.

Colored bars provide a key to the color-coded group

...black ...t, or ...can live for ...store enough ...illions of eggs ...time. Male ants, ...short lives and ...ng.

21–28 days — Female ***Anopheles*** **mosquitoes** suck blood from other animals, which they then digest and use to nourish their eggs. In doing so, these mosquitoes spread deadly diseases such as malaria and elephantiasis between animals.

21 days — **Butterflies** only live for three weeks in their adult form. The common blue butterfly (*top*) has many habitats—forest, downland, sand dunes, and grassy areas. It shares these characteristics with the small skipper (*left*), the American copper (*center*), and the holly blue (*right*).

WHY ARE BUTTERFLIES DIFFERENT COLORS?
Butterflies use their colors for camouflage, to attract mates, and to warn off predators.

? box answers a frequently asked question about one of the species on the spread

YEARS | **50 YEARS** | **75 YEARS** | **100 YEARS** | **200 YEARS** | **500 YEARS** | **1,000 YEARS** | **5,000 YEARS**

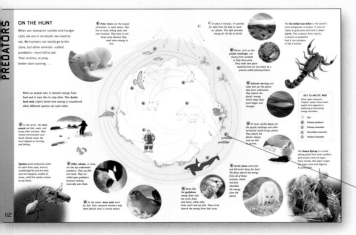

PREDATORS

ON THE HUNT

Feature spreads examine a particular theme or topic in the natural world. Sometimes these pages include maps that show the worldwide distribution of a particular topic. Others may feature a diagram explaining how a particular process or system works.

Some feature spreads include numbered circles. Find the numbered text for an explanation.

112

INTRODUCTION

We share our crowded planet with millions of other species, and each one of their lives is very different. Some species survive for just a few minutes or days and need to make the most of the limited time that they have. *Salmonella enterica* live for less than 30 minutes, but these bacteria can make us sick for weeks at a time. Other organisms might exist for millennia—some trees and coral reefs are thousands of years old.

In *The Kingfisher Encyclopedia of Life*, we explore the extraordinary lives of the animals and plants around us and find out just how different they are from us. We take a look at Labord's chameleon, which spends most of its life locked away in an egg. We peer at the periodical cicada, which lurks underground for 17 years before burrowing up to the surface—only to die within weeks. We consider how the gases produced by kangaroos could help save our planet, and we marvel at the jellyfish that seems to live forever. In addition to presenting a large range of separate species, this book explores how we all exist together and the issues that affect our lives.

This encyclopedia celebrates the color, diversity, and variety of life on Earth in all its many forms. I hope that these pages will inspire readers to respect and conserve the species around them.

Graham L. Banes

1

1-12 MONTHS

ONCE UPON A TIME . . .

Most scientists agree that life began around 3.8 billion years ago, when many different chemicals in a "primordial soup" joined together to make living microorganisms. Over time, these are thought to have evolved, or changed, into the millions of different species that we see on Earth today.

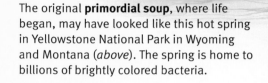

Dinosaurs are believed to have roamed on Earth from around 230 million years ago. This **Tyrannosaurus rex** was among the fiercest of them all.

The original **primordial soup**, where life began, may have looked like this hot spring in Yellowstone National Park in Wyoming and Montana (*above*). The spring is home to billions of brightly colored bacteria.

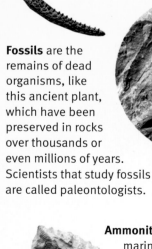

Fossils are the remains of dead organisms, like this ancient plant, which have been preserved in rocks over thousands or even millions of years. Scientists that study fossils are called paleontologists.

Ammonites were ancient marine invertebrates. Most ammonites became extinct at the end of the Cretaceous period: this means that their fossils are more than 65 million years old.

1. **3,800 million years ago (mya)** Simple single-celled microorganisms (prokaryotes) are the first life forms on Earth.

2. **3,500 mya** The last "universal ancestor" in existence, from which all living species are descended.

3. **1,850 mya** More complex single-celled microorganisms (eukaryotes) form.

4. **1,200 mya** Organisms start to reproduce sexually. Multicellular organisms evolve.

5. **580–540 mya** Ozone layer forms and blocks harmful UV rays, allowing organisms to colonize land.

6. **580–500 mya** Cambrian explosion. Most major groups of species evolve.

7. **530 mya** The first known animal footprints on land.

8. **434 mya** Primitive plants and fungi colonize land.

9. **395 mya** The first known tetrapod (four-legged vertebrate) walks on land.

10. **230 mya** Earliest dinosaurs roam on Earth, and the first mammals evolve.

11. **155 mya** First blood-sucking insects.

12. **130 mya** Flowering plants, or angiosperms, dominate the land.

13. **7 mya** The first hominin, or early human, evolves.

14. **4.8 mya** Mammoths appear in the fossil record.

15. **200,000 years ago** Early modern humans, Homo sapiens, appear in Africa.

This timeline shows how **life has evolved** since Earth was formed. Over billions of years, older species have evolved into new ones.

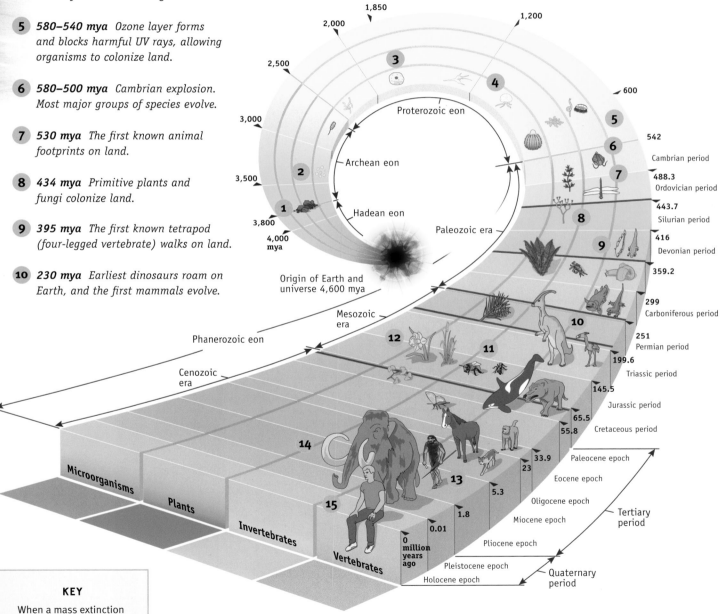

KEY

When a mass extinction occurs, the majority of species on Earth are killed. Asteroid impacts or climate change might cause this to happen.

— **Mass extinctions**

Scientists can learn the age of a **fossilized dinosaur** by looking at the rocks around it. They perform a test, called radiometric dating, which tells them how old the rocks are.

A DAY IN THE LIFE

Many of the oldest and most primitive forms of life are microscopic and consist only of a single cell. Although they have existed on Earth for many millions of years, they live for just a few minutes or hours. Other organisms are more complex and are made up of many cells, but some still live for just a few hours or days.

20–50 minutes In ideal conditions, *Lactococcus lactis* will split in half every 20–50 minutes, producing two new cells. These bacteria are used in the production of butter and cheese.

MICROORGANISMS
PLANTS AND FUNGI
INVERTEBRATES
VERTEBRATES

30 minutes *Salmonella enterica* (*shown red below*) are fast-breeding bacteria. Each cell divides every 30 minutes, so a single bacterium can produce over one million cells in less than a day. They are often found on food and in kitchens. If hands and cooking utensils are not properly cleaned, these bacteria can cause vomiting, diarrhea, and fever.

6 days **Gastrotrichs** are tiny waterborne creatures that feed on single-celled organisms such as algae and amoebas. They are unusual because most gastrotrichs are hermaphrodites, meaning that they have both male and female sex organs.

10–18 hours *Chlamydomonas reinhardtii* are green algae. They can produce hydrogen, which scientists hope to harvest and use as a fuel.

WE ARE HERE

| I MONTH | I YEAR | 2 YEARS | 5 YEARS | IO YEARS | 20 YEARS | 30 YEARS | 50 YEARS |

1–24 hours The **mayfly**, or dayfly, is the only insect to have a winged form (the "subimago") before its adult ("imago") form. The imago's life span is sometimes less than one day, but the mayfly's entire life cycle from egg to imago may be more than a year.

6 days **Mites** (*above*) are members of the spider family (Arachnida). Some mites are parasites, living on larger animals and plants. Mites can cause allergies in humans and spread serious infections.

10–18 hours The larvae of the **Pindi moth** of Australia feed on the roots of the eucalyptus tree. They live for up to 18 months, but the adult moth lives for less than a day, partially because it has no mouth and cannot eat.

12–36 hours Some *Coprinus* **mushrooms** have no chlorophyll, the green substance by which a plant produces starch and sugar. The part that we see, known as the fruiting body, is a delicate structure that can grow overnight, but lives for only a day or two before collapsing.

AMOEBAS

Among the simplest microorganisms on Earth, amoebas are bloblike, single-celled life forms that live in water. For such simple creatures, amoebas have some remarkable characteristics: in particular, they can change their shape continually. An amoeba is made up of a jellylike structure and moves around by extending parts of its body ("pseudopods") forward, into which the rest of its body then flows. This shape-shifting ability helps an amoeba feed—it wraps its body around other microorganisms and engulfs its prey. To reproduce, each amoeba divides itself within around 24 hours into two new cells. These cells are genetically identical.

MICROORGANISMS

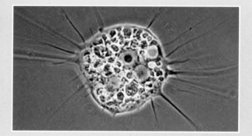

A **protective chemical barrier** is produced by amoebas to defend them from predators.

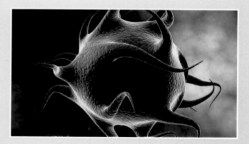

With up to **670 billion units of DNA**, amoebas have 231 times more than the human genome.

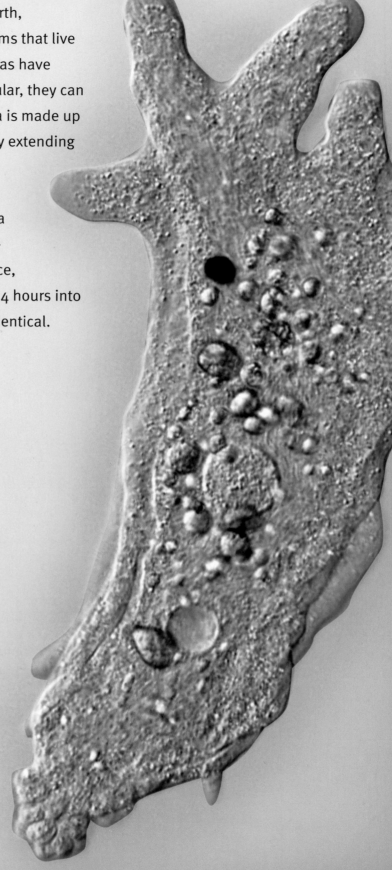

Amoeba proteus

BUSY FOR THE NEXT THREE WEEKS

A lot of busy and familiar insects and microorganisms perform their useful tasks within a life span of less than one month. There are others that, in the same time, can spread unpleasant diseases far and wide.

7–21 days The **fly agaric mushroom** is found in woodlands all over the world. This toadstool lives for up to three weeks. It reproduces by dispersing fungal spores, which grow into clones of itself.

3–45 days There are almost 2,000 species of **rotifers**, varying in size from under one-tenth of a millimeter to just 2mm. They live in the sea and fresh water and form an important part of the plankton that many fish feed upon.

MICROORGANISMS
PLANTS AND FUNGI
INVERTEBRATES
VERTEBRATES

12–22 days **Wasps** build their nests from wood, paper, and cardboard that they chew to make a kind of cement. The largest wasps' nest ever recorded was found on a farm in New Zealand, with a diameter of more than 5.75 ft. (1.75m).

14–21 days **Nematodes**, or roundworms, live in every type of habitat on Earth. They are the most abundant in water and make up more than 90 percent of all life at the bottom of the oceans.

14–21 days A female **black garden ant**, or princess, can live for up to 15 years and store enough sperm to fertilize millions of eggs throughout her lifetime. Male ants, or drones, live very short lives and die soon after mating.

14–30 days **Houseflies** feed on rotting flesh and feces (poop). They spit saliva onto their food to liquefy it, then suck it up using an extendable mouth called a proboscis.

| 1 MONTH | 1 YEAR | 2 YEARS | 5 YEARS | 10 YEARS | 20 YEARS | 30 YEARS | 50 YEARS |

14–30 days **Spider mites** often invade crops, feeding on fruit and vegetables.

30 days The **Australian shield shrimp** is a small crustacean. It is a living fossil—it hasn't changed at all for more than 200 million years. Adult shrimp have three eyes, one of which may be light-sensitive.

DO NOT TOUCH!
Although it is very pretty, the fly agaric mushroom is highly dangerous to eat and should never be touched.

21–28 days Female ***Anopheles*** **mosquitoes** suck blood from other animals, which they then digest and use to nourish their eggs. In doing so, these mosquitoes spread deadly diseases such as malaria and elephantiasis between animals.

21 days **Butterflies** only live for three weeks in their adult form. The common blue butterfly (*top*) has many habitats—forest, downland, sand dunes, and grassy areas. It shares these characteristics with the small skipper (*left*), the American copper (*center*), and the holly blue (*right*).

WHY ARE BUTTERFLIES DIFFERENT COLORS?

Butterflies use their colors for camouflage, to attract mates, and to warn off predators.

75 YEARS   **100 YEARS**   **200 YEARS**   **500 YEARS**   **1,000 YEARS**   **5,000 YEARS**

INVERTEBRATES

Honeybees live in **nests**, sometimes called hives, which they build from beeswax. Bees naturally produce this wax from special glands on their bodies.

The **queen bee** is the largest female in the colony, and the only female who is able to have offspring. She is usually the mother of all of the other bees in the nest.

| I MONTH | I YEAR | 2 YEARS | 5 YEARS | 10 YEARS | 20 YEARS | 30 YEARS | 50 YEARS |

HONEYBEES

Honeybees live in a very complex society that revolves around a single queen bee. Male drone bees have to mate with the queen, producing new offspring to increase the colony's population. Unlike the queen, female worker bees cannot have any offspring and spend much of their time building and taking care of the nest. These workers also collect plant pollen and nectar for food, and when doing so, they transfer pollen from one plant to another. This process, called pollination, plays a vital role in plant fertilization. The number of bees worldwide has been declining in recent years, however, possibly due to an unknown disease. Scientists are concerned that fewer bees will mean less pollination. This could have a disastrous effect on plant biodiversity and food production.

75 YEARS   100 YEARS   200 YEARS   500 YEARS   1,000 YEARS   5,000 YEARS

YEARNING FOR A YEAR

We all know how it feels to want something that we can't have. These species might like to live for a year, but few of them even come close. Most of their life spans are very short and are over after just a few months.

1–2 months In less than one month, 25 **human flea** females can produce more than 250,000 flea offspring. At one time, most of Europe was infested, with almost everyone carrying fleas. Today, better hygiene has restricted the human flea to cats, dogs, and pigs.

1–3 months Hungry **dermestid beetles** and their larvae (*below*) enjoy eating raw flesh. They are often used by museum staff to help clean skulls and bones for display.

MICROORGANISMS
PLANTS AND FUNGI
INVERTEBRATES
VERTEBRATES

2–3 months The **meadow vole** lives across much of North America, ranging as far north as the Arctic. Voles that live in colder climates grow to be much larger than those in warmer areas. Their bigger bodies help them store more warmth and energy.

2 months The light produced by a **firefly** is the most efficient light in the world, because it produces very little heat. This "cold" light is 30 times more energy-efficient than the average electric light bulb that you might find at home.

| MONTH | | YEAR | | 2 YEARS | 5 YEARS | 10 YEARS | 20 YEARS | 30 YEARS | 50 YEARS |

6–12 months **European badgers** are nocturnal, meaning that they sleep during the day and are active at night. They live in underground burrows called sets, which are made up of many different tunnels and chambers. Although badgers can live for up to 15 years, most die from diseases or in accidents after just a few months.

3 months The **tsetse fly** is a large, brown, biting fly that feeds on the blood of vertebrates, including humans. It transmits diseases such as sleeping sickness. Without treatment, a bite from an infected fly could kill a person in months.

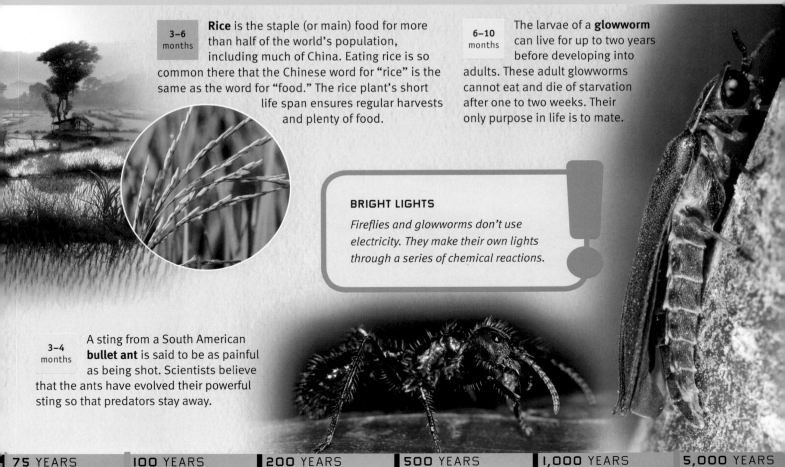

3–6 months **Rice** is the staple (or main) food for more than half of the world's population, including much of China. Eating rice is so common there that the Chinese word for "rice" is the same as the word for "food." The rice plant's short life span ensures regular harvests and plenty of food.

6–10 months The larvae of a **glowworm** can live for up to two years before developing into adults. These adult glowworms cannot eat and die of starvation after one to two weeks. Their only purpose in life is to mate.

BRIGHT LIGHTS

Fireflies and glowworms don't use electricity. They make their own lights through a series of chemical reactions.

3–4 months A sting from a South American **bullet ant** is said to be as painful as being shot. Scientists believe that the ants have evolved their powerful sting so that predators stay away.

75 YEARS   **100 YEARS**   **200 YEARS**   **500 YEARS**   **1,000 YEARS**   **5,000 YEARS**

INVERTEBRATES

1 MONTH | 1 YEAR | 2 YEARS | 5 YEARS | 10 YEARS | 20 YEARS | 30 YEARS | 50 YEARS

LEAF-CUTTER ANTS

Young leaf-cutter ants begin their lives with razorlike jaws that vibrate 1,000 times per second to cut off pieces of a leaf. Older ants, whose teeth have worn down during the course of their life span, then carry the leaf pieces back to their colony. A single colony can house up to eight million ants.

Leaf-cutter ants use the leaves that they collect to feed a **special fungus**. This fungus is then eaten by the ant larvae.

Each ant can carry **more than 20 times its own body weight**—that's equivalent to a human carrying a small car.

A CROWDED PLANET

Life comes in all different shapes and sizes and can be found in every corner of our planet. Some parts of the world are more biodiverse than others, meaning that they are home to a greater number and variety of species. These crowded areas are called biodiversity hot spots, and they play host to some extraordinary organisms.

1 Around 2,000 species of plants grow only in California—and nowhere else in the world. This **giant sequoia** is the world's largest tree.

2 The islands of the Pacific Ocean are home to many endemic (or native) species. This plant, the **silversword**, can only be found on the slopes of Hawaii's highest volcanoes.

NORTH AMERICA

PACIFIC OCEAN

ATLANTIC OCEAN

1 California

2 Hawaiian Islands

3 Amazonia

SOUTH AMERICA

Brazil **4**

HOW OFTEN ARE NEW SPECIES DISCOVERED?

More than 18,000 new species are discovered every year. That's two new species per hour.

3 The Amazonian tropical rainforest is the largest in the world. It is so big that it spans nine countries. Many millions of different insects live in the Amazon, including this **spiny bush cricket**.

Animals living on islands often grow to giant sizes over time. This New Zealand **giant weta** has few predators and does not need to be small enough to hide.

4 Deforestation is a big problem in Brazil's Atlantic forest, which has already been cut to 10 percent of its original size. This is very worrying for the **golden lion tamarin**, as only 1,000 are left in the wild.

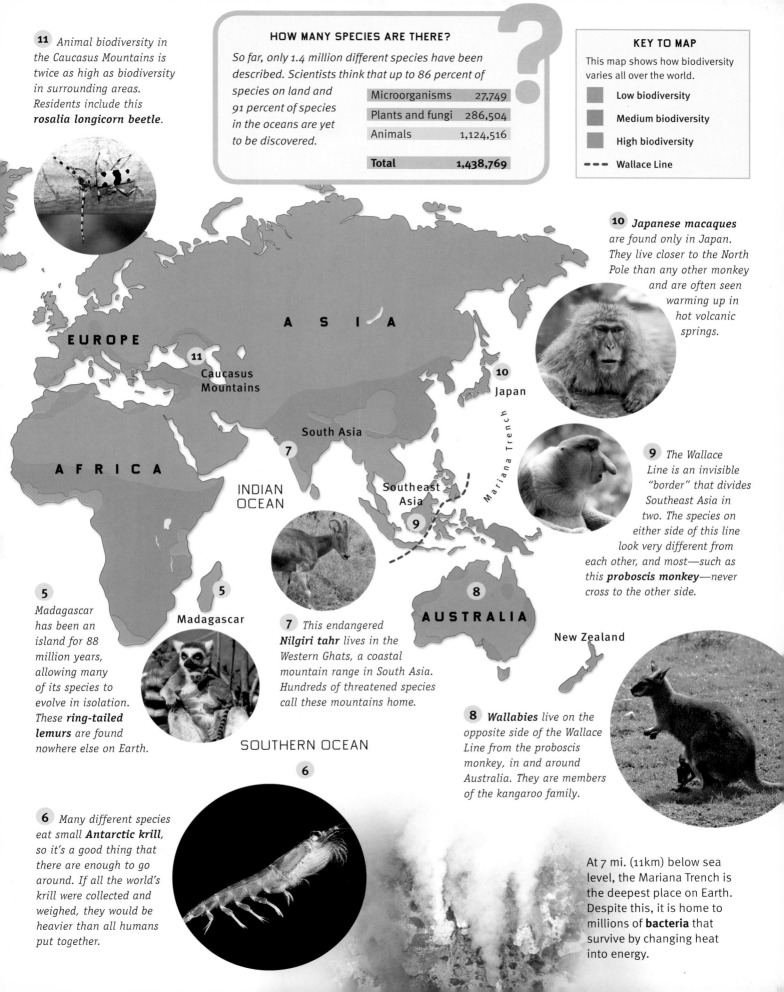

11 Animal biodiversity in the Caucasus Mountains is twice as high as biodiversity in surrounding areas. Residents include this **rosalia longicorn beetle**.

KEY TO MAP

This map shows how biodiversity varies all over the world.

- Low biodiversity
- Medium biodiversity
- High biodiversity
- - - - Wallace Line

10 **Japanese macaques** are found only in Japan. They live closer to the North Pole than any other monkey and are often seen warming up in hot volcanic springs.

9 The Wallace Line is an invisible "border" that divides Southeast Asia in two. The species on either side of this line look very different from each other, and most—such as this **proboscis monkey**—never cross to the other side.

5 Madagascar has been an island for 88 million years, allowing many of its species to evolve in isolation. These **ring-tailed lemurs** are found nowhere else on Earth.

7 This endangered **Nilgiri tahr** lives in the Western Ghats, a coastal mountain range in South Asia. Hundreds of threatened species call these mountains home.

8 **Wallabies** live on the opposite side of the Wallace Line from the proboscis monkey, in and around Australia. They are members of the kangaroo family.

6 Many different species eat small **Antarctic krill**, so it's a good thing that there are enough to go around. If all the world's krill were collected and weighed, they would be heavier than all humans put together.

At 7 mi. (11km) below sea level, the Mariana Trench is the deepest place on Earth. Despite this, it is home to millions of **bacteria** that survive by changing heat into energy.

EUROPE

ASIA

AFRICA

Caucasus Mountains

South Asia

INDIAN OCEAN

Southeast Asia

Japan

Mariana Trench

Madagascar

AUSTRALIA

New Zealand

SOUTHERN OCEAN

CLOSER TO CAKE

Birthday celebrations are on the horizon, and where there's a party, there's cake. If they're lucky, some of these species might live long enough to savor a piece, but don't light the candles just yet. It's more likely that their life spans will fall just short of a year.

6 months The complete life cycle of a **dragonfly** normally lasts for six months, but some larger dragonflies can live for seven years. Dragonflies can fly at speeds of up to 30 mph (50km/h)—that's about five times faster than a running human.

MICROORGANISMS
PLANTS AND FUNGI
INVERTEBRATES
VERTEBRATES

6 months It's easy to grow your own **peanut plant** from raw, uncooked peanuts planted 2 in. (5cm) deep in soil. Your plant should start to grow within a week, and peanuts should appear within three months. A soccer field could grow enough plants to make 45,000 peanut-butter sandwiches.

6–12 months The venom (poison) sac of a male **black widow spider** stops growing at an early age. Females produce high quantities of venom throughout their entire life spans and are very dangerous spiders. The bright-red hourglass on their black stomach warns predators to stay away.

WILL A WIDOW KILL ME?
Humans rarely die from black widow bites, but full recovery can take a week or more.

| 1 MONTH | 1 YEAR | 2 YEARS | 5 YEARS | 10 YEARS | 20 YEARS | 30 YEARS | 50 YEARS |

10–12 months A **praying mantis** is well equipped to search for prey: it has five eyes that can see as far as 60 ft. (18m) and is able to turn its head almost completely around in a circle. Males should be wary of hungry females, however—during mating, the female mantis sometimes bites off the male's head and eats it.

INSECT INVASION!

The praying mantis comes from Europe and was introduced to North America by accident. Despite being an invasive species, the praying mantis has been appointed the state insect of Connecticut.

11 months The **brown antechinus** lives in the forests of eastern Australia. In warm weather, these animals sleep alone. When it is colder, females work together to build large nests that are shared by many individuals. Though females can live for up to three years, males die within just 12 months from the stress and exhaustion of mating.

12 months **Brine shrimp**, or sea monkeys, are often kept as pets. Although their life cycle only lasts for one year, a brine shrimp's eggs can survive for several years before hatching. The eggs can cope without water and oxygen, survive boiling-hot and freezing-cold temperatures, and still hatch into healthy shrimp.

12 months The **garden strawberry** was created in France in 1740 by crossbreeding two different species of wild strawberries. For this reason it is called a hybrid, because its parents came from two different species. Strawberries are the only fruit with seeds on the outside, instead of inside. The average strawberry has 200 seeds.

10 months The **bedbug** is an unwelcome house guest, sucking on the blood of sleeping humans. Bedbugs hide in mattresses, bed frames, and other furniture, coming out at night to feed.

JELLYFISH

A jellyfish has no brain, heart, or eyes, and more than 90 percent of its body is made up of water. Despite this, these impressive invertebrates have colonized every ocean in the world, from the surface to the bottom of the deepest sea. The lion's mane jellyfish is the largest on Earth and lives in the Arctic, Atlantic, and Pacific oceans. Its tentacles can grow as long as 120 ft. (36.5m)—longer than three school buses.

Lion's mane jellyfish

INVERTEBRATES

| I MONTH | I YEAR | 2 YEARS | 5 YEARS | IO YEARS | 20 YEARS | 30 YEARS | 50 YEARS |

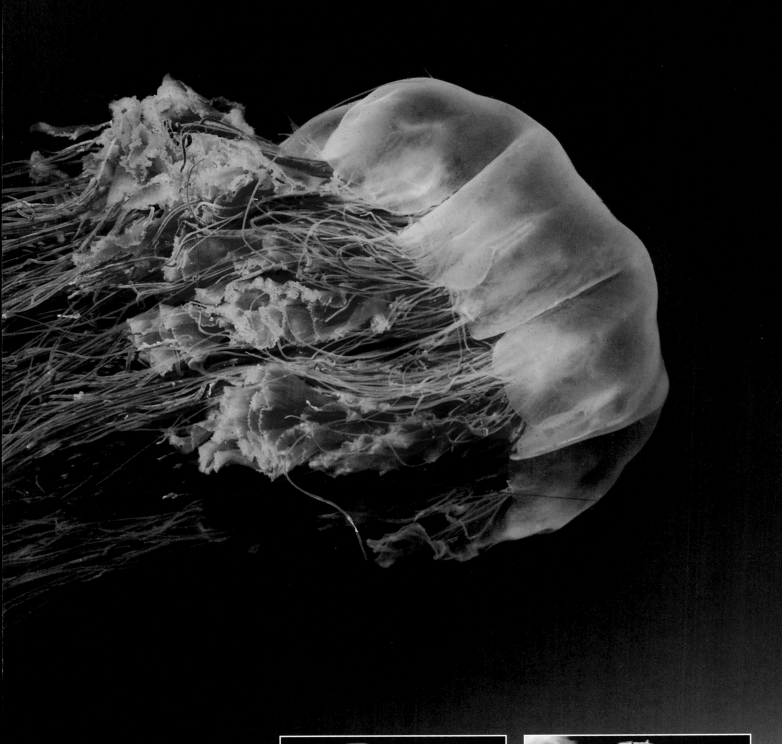

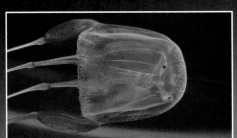

*A single box jellyfish contains enough **lethal venom** to kill up to 60 adult humans.*

*The flower hat jellyfish **grows or shrinks**, depending on how much food there is.*

THERE'S NO PLACE LIKE HOME

Every species has basic needs, such as food and shelter. We normally find these things in the space that we choose to live in. This space is our home, and it is called our habitat. Each habitat has different features that meet the needs of the species that live there.

1 *Coniferous forests* cover colder regions and are made up of evergreen trees that have green leaves on them all year round. These leaves are constantly replaced.

There are no plants or sunlight at such depths, but plenty of other species call the **deep oceans** home. They feed mostly on decaying animals that have died near the surface and sunk to the seabed.

IT'S NOT CHILE HERE!

Chile's Atacama Desert is so hot that its rivers have been dry for 120,000 years.

PACIFIC OCEAN

NORTH AMERICA

ATLANTIC OCEAN

SOUTH AMERICA

ATACAMA DESERT

2 *Deserts* are very dry areas that rarely receive any rain. Most species that live in deserts stay hidden during the day in order to keep cool and to avoid drying out.

KEY TO MAP

This map shows the types and locations of the different habitats that can be found all over the world.

- Arctic and tundra
- Coniferous forest
- Deciduous forest
- Grassland and savanna
- Desert
- Mediterranean
- Tropical forest

Coastlines are rich and varied habitats with many different places to live. Birds can be found nesting in rocky cliffs, crabs can hide in tidal pools, and seaweed can thrive on the shoreline.

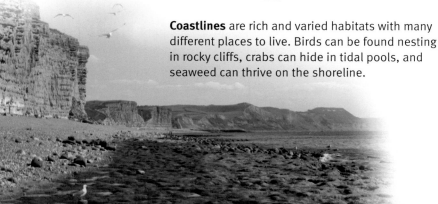

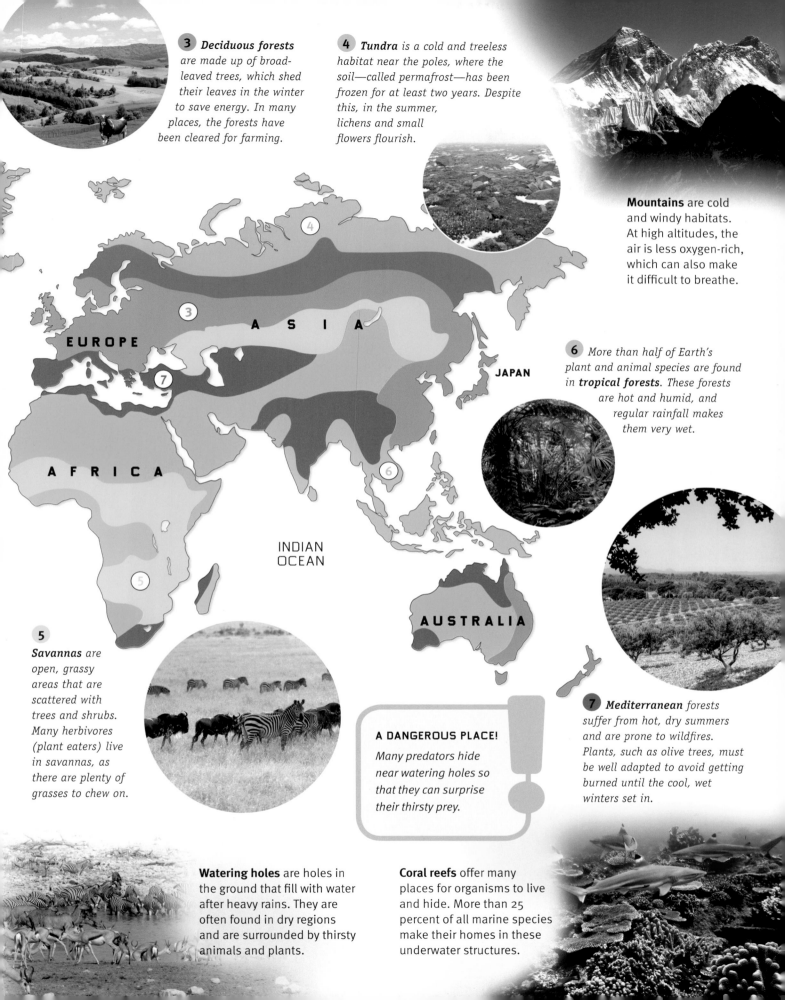

3 *Deciduous forests* are made up of broad-leaved trees, which shed their leaves in the winter to save energy. In many places, the forests have been cleared for farming.

4 *Tundra* is a cold and treeless habitat near the poles, where the soil—called permafrost—has been frozen for at least two years. Despite this, in the summer, lichens and small flowers flourish.

Mountains are cold and windy habitats. At high altitudes, the air is less oxygen-rich, which can also make it difficult to breathe.

EUROPE

A S I A

AFRICA

JAPAN

INDIAN OCEAN

AUSTRALIA

6 More than half of Earth's plant and animal species are found in **tropical forests**. These forests are hot and humid, and regular rainfall makes them very wet.

5 *Savannas* are open, grassy areas that are scattered with trees and shrubs. Many herbivores (plant eaters) live in savannas, as there are plenty of grasses to chew on.

A DANGEROUS PLACE!
Many predators hide near watering holes so that they can surprise their thirsty prey.

7 *Mediterranean* forests suffer from hot, dry summers and are prone to wildfires. Plants, such as olive trees, must be well adapted to avoid getting burned until the cool, wet winters set in.

Watering holes are holes in the ground that fill with water after heavy rains. They are often found in dry regions and are surrounded by thirsty animals and plants.

Coral reefs offer many places for organisms to live and hide. More than 25 percent of all marine species make their homes in these underwater structures.

The **atlas moth** is the largest moth in the world, with a wingspan of up to 12 in. (30cm)—about as wide as a laptop computer. Adult atlas moths live only for two weeks and do not eat at all during that time. Instead, they digest the supplies of fat that they stored when they were caterpillars.

Slave-making ants steal the offspring of other ant species and raise them to be their slaves. The slave ants are forced to forage for food and to maintain the nest in order to keep the queen ant happy.

Darwin's bark spider was discovered in Madagascar in 2010, sitting in a massive web 82 ft. (25m) across—longer than two school buses parked end to end. The silk that it produces to build its web is the strongest material known to humans. It is 50 times stronger than the strongest steel and ten times tougher than a bulletproof vest.

The NASA space shuttle *Discovery* was launched into orbit on February 24, 2011 with some rather unsavory passengers: a whole host of harmful **bacteria**. Scientists hope to study how dangerous superbugs are affected by zero-gravity conditions. This could help us fight bacteria back on Earth.

The **cat flea** can jump as high as 13 in. (34cm) in a single leap, accelerating 20 times faster than a space rocket.

1-10 YEARS

GET THE PARTY STARTED

It was tough, but they made it. Despite all the trials of early life, each of these species has made it to a year and all can celebrate at least one birthday. Some might even make it to two!

12–14 months After spending between eight and nine months developing in the egg, the **Labord's chameleon** of Madagascar has the shortest-known life span of any land-living, four-limbed vertebrate, or "tetrapod"—only four to five months. Having hatched and grown to maturity in just eight weeks, these chameleons mate and die off as the tropical dry season sets in.

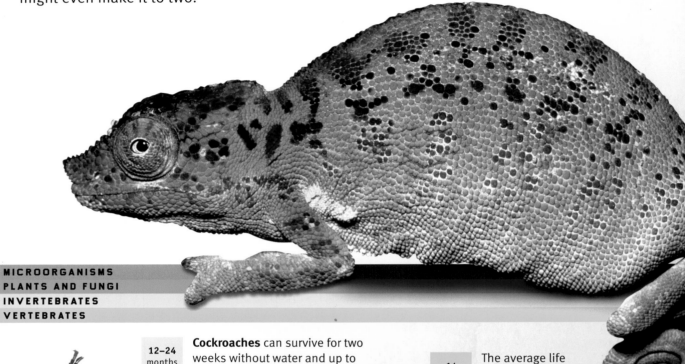

MICROORGANISMS
PLANTS AND FUNGI
INVERTEBRATES
VERTEBRATES

12–24 months **Cockroaches** can survive for two weeks without water and up to four weeks without food. They often thrive where humans live, eating the remains of our meals. They wallow in dirt and spread diseases.

DON'T LOSE YOUR HEAD!
A cockroach can live for up to a week without its head before it starves to death.

14 months The average life span of a **European robin** is much lower than that of most garden birds: only 20 percent reach adulthood. Those that survive defend their territory fiercely, especially in the winter when food is scarce. Larger, tougher birds attack and kill robins, cutting short their life span.

12–18 months The **common house mouse** is a nocturnal animal, sleeping during the day. Mice are an important food for small predatory animals, reptiles, and birds. Pet mice are descended from wild mice and can live up to six years.

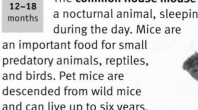

1 MONTH | 1 YEAR | 2 YEARS | 5 YEARS | 10 YEARS | 20 YEARS | 30 YEARS | 50 YEARS

DO CARROTS MAKE YOU SEE IN THE DARK?

Actually, they don't. This myth was created during World War II, when food rationing in Europe meant that any way of getting people to eat vegetables was encouraged.

24 months We pick **carrots** to eat in their first year, but they have a two-year life cycle. If left in the ground, they flower, set seed, and then die in their second year. The same is true for some other vegetables such as parsnips, beets, and celery.

18–36 months All **ladybugs** start life as shiny yellow eggs that hatch into spiky, black, six-legged larvae. The larvae turn into pupae, from which adult ladybugs emerge. An adult female can lay more than 1,000 eggs in the spring and summer, before hibernating in the winter. Estimates of the ladybug's life span vary greatly, depending on climate, the environment, and predators.

24 months Up to 90 percent of wild **European rabbits** die in their first year, largely due to disease, predators, and human impact. Domestic rabbits can live much longer, and with proper care and feeding a pet rabbit may live for ten years.

12–14 months The **mourning cloak butterfly**, or Camberwell beauty, lives in colder regions of Europe, Asia, and North America. It can survive subzero temperatures because it produces a natural antifreeze.

24 months **Honesty** is a biennial plant that originally comes from western Asia. It is grown for its decorative flowers and the flattened seedpods that grow in its second year of life. These look like coins, hence its nicknames: the "money plant" or "silver dollars."

24 months The freshwater **mosquitofish** lives in Central and North America and eats the larvae and pupae of mosquitoes. Scientists have introduced the fish all around the world as a way to control malaria-carrying mosquito populations. This natural method, called biological control, avoids the use of harmful pesticides.

75 YEARS   **100** YEARS   **200** YEARS   **500** YEARS   **1,000** YEARS   **5,000** YEARS

PLANTS AND FUNGI

I MONTH | I YEAR | 2 YEARS | 5 YEARS | I0 YEARS | 20 YEARS | 30 YEARS | 50 YEARS

ANNUAL PLANTS

Annual plants, such as the sunflower, are those that germinate, flower, and die in less than one year. Sunflowers are named after their bright yellow heads, which resemble a blazing sun. Each sunflower head is made up of more than a thousand individual flowers joined together. Despite their short lives, sunflowers can grow very fast and reach heights of up to 26 ft. (8m).

*Because they grow so rapidly, annual plants can quickly **transform barren landscapes** into pretty and colorful gardens.*

***Many of our clothes** are made from upland cotton, an annual plant that has been cultivated for 5,000 years.*

SEE YOU NEXT CHRISTMAS?

Maybe not. For some species that live for more than one year—which normally means surviving a winter—the second year is their last. These species include small animals such as the pheasant and red fox, whose average life spans are made much shorter by human activities that disrupt their habitats—hunting, farming, and careless driving, for example.

10–12 months The larvae of the **eastern goliath beetle** are the heaviest insects on Earth, weighing in at up to 3.5 oz. (100g)—the same as a small banana. Adult beetles grow up to 4 in. (11cm) long and can be seen in the rainforests of tropical Africa.

MICROORGANISMS
PLANTS AND FUNGI
INVERTEBRATES
VERTEBRATES

1–2 years With a length of 22.3 in. (56.7cm), **Chan's megastick** is the world's longest insect. This stick insect is new to science, and only three specimens have been found so far, all in Malaysian Borneo.

2 years Female **deer ticks** attach themselves to white-tailed deer, drinking their blood for up to a week. Once full, a female tick lays as many as 3,000 eggs.

2 years **Pheasants** are sexually dimorphic, meaning that males and females are very different in appearance. Their brains are the same small size, however, and most are outwitted by predators before the age of three.

| MONTH | 1 YEAR | 2 YEARS | 5 YEARS | 10 YEARS | 20 YEARS | 30 YEARS | 50 YEARS |

1–2 years When frightened, the **Caribbean reef squid** can jet propel itself out of the water and "fly" up to 33 ft. (10m) across the ocean—a distance 50 times longer than its own body.

1.5 years The average wild **red fox** will not live to be two years old. Most foxes are killed in car accidents or by people who consider them pests.

2 years Instead of giving trophies at the Olympic Games, the ancient Greeks presented winners with wreaths of **parsley**. Today, parsley is commonly used in cooking.

2 years The leaves, flowers, and seeds of the **foxglove** are all poisonous to humans and many animals. Each plant contains enough poison to kill an adult man.

15–16 months Tiny **pygmy shrews** weigh less than a teaspoon of sugar. Because their small size means that they cannot store food, these shrews eat every two hours in order to stay alive.

ETERNAL TEA TIME
Many people die drinking tea made from foxglove, not realizing the plant is poisonous.

1–2 years The flowers of **sheep's bit scabious** glow bright red under ultraviolet light. This light is invisible to humans, but can be seen by some flying insects. They are attracted to the color and help pollinate the plant.

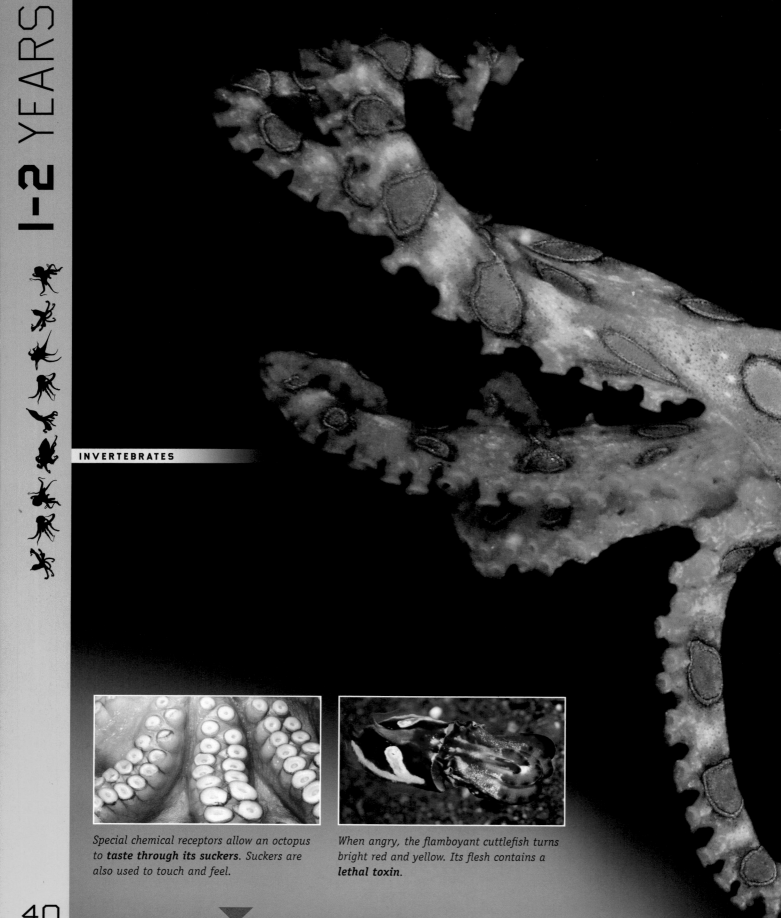

INVERTEBRATES

Special chemical receptors allow an octopus to **taste through its suckers**. Suckers are also used to touch and feel.

When angry, the flamboyant cuttlefish turns bright red and yellow. Its flesh contains a **lethal toxin**.

1 MONTH	1 YEAR	2 YEARS	5 YEARS	10 YEARS	20 YEARS	30 YEARS	50 YEARS

OCTOPUSES

Octopuses and cuttlefish are cephalopods—molluscs with a large head and a beaklike mouth ringed by sucker-tipped arms. The blue-ringed octopus is found in the Pacific Ocean and is one of the world's deadliest animals, even though it is only the size of a tennis ball. When angry, dozens of electric-blue rings appear on its yellowish skin and appear to "glow" brightly. The octopus then injects its venomous saliva into passing prey, paralyzing it instantly. Although this octopus normally preys on small crustaceans, its venom is deadly enough to kill a human within minutes.

75 YEARS | 100 YEARS | 200 YEARS | 500 YEARS | 1,000 YEARS | 5,000 YEARS

STRONGER THAN YESTERDAY

They've survived for at least two years, and they're bigger, brighter, and bolder than before. If these species can find enough food and stay out of trouble, some could live for up to five years. After all, what doesn't kill us makes us stronger . . .

WATCH OUT!

A squirt from a skunk can travel up to 10 ft. (3m).

2–3 years When threatened, a **striped skunk** squirts out a foul-smelling acid from the scent glands outside its anus (bottom). This liquid burns the eyes of unfortunate predators.

MICROORGANISMS
PLANTS AND FUNGI
INVERTEBRATES
VERTEBRATES

2.5 years The **pill bug**, or wood louse, isn't an insect—it's actually a crustacean. Pill bugs are more closely related to lobsters than to insects.

2–3 years North American **raccoons** are opportunistic feeders, eating whatever is convenient at the time. They are happy to raid garbage cans and steal food from houses, which can make them unpopular with humans.

3 years **Dung beetles** roll dung (poop) into giant balls, then suck out the dung's juices and drink them. Females lay their eggs inside the dung.

I WANT MY BALL BACK!

Dung balls need to be buried in secret to stop other dung beetles from stealing them.

I MONTH | I YEAR | 2 YEARS | 5 YEARS | IO YEARS | 20 YEARS | 30 YEARS | 50 YEARS

3 years The **arctic fox** lives in the arctic tundra and can even be found at the North Pole. Its thick fur and body fat protect it from ice and help it survive in freezing temperatures.

2–4 years **Virginia opossums** have 50 sharp teeth and hiss and growl when threatened. They are North America's only marsupials—animals whose offspring are kept in a pouch.

DOES "GOLIATH" EAT BIRDS?

Goliath "bird-eating" spiders were given their name after early explorers saw one eat a hummingbird. Their usual diet is made up of insects.

3–6 years The **goliath bird-eating spider** lives in the tropical rainforests of South America. It is one of the largest spiders in the world, with a leg span of up to 12 in. (30.5cm)—about the size of a dinner plate. Its huge fangs can grow as long as 1.5 in. (3.8cm). Although females can live to 25, males die within just six years.

3–5 years **Passion flowers** are commercially farmed, with a life span of three to five years. Their sweet-tasting passion fruit are used to make delicious drinks and desserts.

MOLES

It may not win a beauty pageant, but the star-nosed mole has other talents. Its star-shaped nose, made up of 22 pink and fleshy tentacles, contains 25,000 touch receptors that help the mole feel its way around. This incredible sense of touch allows the mole to identify and devour its food in just 120 milliseconds—faster than any other mammal on Earth. Many species of moles also have toxic saliva, which they use to paralyze earthworms. They store these earthworms for later, when they are hungry enough to eat them.

VERTEBRATES

*All moles are blind and live underground. They use their **huge claws** to dig extensive tunnels.*

__Molehills__ are mounds of soil that appear when moles dig their way up to the surface.

LIFE'S GOING SWIMMINGLY!

Many species that survive for two to five years are aquatic animals that live in water. Most of these species can only breathe underwater and would die if they were taken out. Others, such as the cane toad and California grunion, have also adapted to life on land.

2–5 years **Sea horses** start life as tiny eggs, produced by the female sea horse. She gives her eggs to a male sea horse, who carries them around for weeks or months before "giving birth" to the offspring.

MICROORGANISMS
PLANTS AND FUNGI
INVERTEBRATES
VERTEBRATES

2–4 years **Siamese fighting fish** (or betta fish) are brightly colored and make popular pets. However, they are so foul tempered that they will even attack their own reflection. Male fish fight to the death and must always be kept alone.

2–4 years Beginning on the nights of the full and new moons, **California grunion** fish crawl out of the ocean to spawn (lay eggs) on beaches.

3–5 years The **North Pacific giant** is the world's largest octopus, weighing up to 157 lb. (71kg)— about the same as an average man. It is thought to be big enough to catch and eat small sharks.

I MONTH   I YEAR   2 YEARS   5 YEARS   IO YEARS   20 YEARS   30 YEARS   50 YEARS

4–6 years

The **Tasmanian pygmy possum** is the world's smallest possum, weighing just 25–35 oz. (7–10g) (about the same as a pencil). To conserve energy in cold weather, this possum breathes 99 percent less oxygen than normal.

4–5 years

Leeches attach themselves to humans and animals with nearly 100 sharp but tiny teeth. They then suck the blood of their unwilling hosts, swelling up and dropping off when full.

CAN LEECHES BE USEFUL?

Doctors have used leeches for more than 2,000 years to release blood and reduce blood pressure.

4–6 years

Sugar gliders get their name from their ability to "fly" through the forests of Australia and Southeast Asia. They can glide up to 148 ft. (45m) using special flaps between their legs that look like wings.

5 years

Cane toads are native to the Americas, but were introduced to Australia in 1935. They have since killed many native species, badly affecting biodiversity.

5 years

Giant African land snails are the largest terrestrial (land-living) snails in the world, weighing just under 2 lb. (1kg)—about the same as a bag of sugar. Their tongues have tiny hooks called radula, which scrape off plant material for the snail to eat.

75 YEARS | **100 YEARS** | **200 YEARS** | **500 YEARS** | **1,000 YEARS** | **5,000 YEARS**

VERTEBRATES

Female rats usually give birth to up to **14 baby rats**, called pups. They have as many as five litters, or sets of offspring, each year.

Wild rats carry **many different diseases**, including swine fever, foot-and-mouth disease, and Weil's disease.

| 1 MONTH | 1 YEAR | 2 YEARS | 5 YEARS | 10 YEARS | 20 YEARS | 30 YEARS | 50 YEARS |

RATS

In some cultures, including much of Europe, rats are thought to be dirty, disease-ridden pests. In others, in parts of Africa and Asia, they are sometimes considered food. In India, rats are believed to be sacred and are important to religious traditions. Regardless of whether you love or hate them, rats are here to stay. In the city of New York alone, there are thought to be more rats than humans. Each of the eight million people within the city limits is believed to live alongside at least one rat.

75 YEARS | 100 YEARS | 200 YEARS | 500 YEARS | 1,000 YEARS | 5,000 YEARS

DETERMINED TO STAY

They may not live for very long, but they certainly do try. All these animals do their best to live a little longer: the red-eyed tree frog startles predators with its crimson eyes, and the guinea pig bites anyone who gets too close. None lives for more than five to ten years, but they're not going down without a fight.

5–7 years

Porcupines are rodents and are covered in up to 30,000 sharp quills that they use to defend themselves from predators. Contrary to popular belief, porcupines cannot "shoot" their quills. Instead, they charge into their enemies and stab them, releasing the quills into the victim's flesh. Each quill is tipped with a barb, or hook, making it difficult to remove.

5 years

Red-eyed tree frogs are arboreal, which means that they live in trees. Their feet are covered in sticky pads that glue these amphibians to branches to stop them from falling.

MICROORGANISMS
PLANTS AND FUNGI
INVERTEBRATES
VERTEBRATES

6 years

Earthworms breathe through their skin by absorbing oxygen from water in the soil. To prevent dehydration, they coat themselves in slimy mucus and live in damp, underground tunnels up to 7 ft. (2m) deep.

5 years

House geckos are found in houses all over Asia and are often kept as pets. When frightened, these reptiles "drop" their tails. The dropped tail wiggles and twitches for several seconds, distracting a predator and allowing the gecko to escape. A new tail can grow back in just four weeks.

HOW LONG DO WORMS GROW?

The longest earthworm ever found measured 22 ft. (6.7m)–three times longer than a giraffe's neck.

I MONTH   I YEAR   2 YEARS   5 YEARS   IO YEARS   20 YEARS   30 YEARS   50 YEARS

NOT A PRETTY FELLOW!

Kingfishers need to eat around 60 percent of their own body weight each day in order to stay alive. They throw their young out of the nest at a very early age, forcing them to find their own food. Adult kingfishers fight fiercely to protect their feeding territories.

7 years

Common kingfishers feed by diving underwater and catching fish at high speed. They bash the fish against their perch to stun or kill it, before swallowing it headfirst. This helps stop any spines along the fish's body from sticking in the kingfisher's throat.

5–10 years

When threatened, **sea cucumbers** (*below*) push out their internal organs and explode sticky threads from their bottom to entangle predators. They can also fit into cracks and crevices by liquefying their bodies and pouring themselves into the empty space.

5–10 years

Acorn barnacles produce a natural cement and glue themselves to rocks at the seashore. When the tide is in, they open their cases and stick out tiny feelers to filter for food. When the tide is out, their hard cases stay firmly closed to protect the barnacles from drying out in the sun.

5–8 years

Guinea pigs live in the wild parts of South America, but are also popular pets. Like humans, they cannot produce their own vitamin C, so they have to eat vegetables in order to survive. Their front teeth never stop growing, and are worn down by the food that they eat.

GRAY WOLVES

Wolves once had the largest natural distribution of any mammal except humans, living across much of the Northern Hemisphere. Today, their range has been reduced by one-third due to human activities. These have also reduced the wolf's life span in the wild to between six and eight years, although some wolves have been known to live for 13 years or more. Wolves live and travel in groups of around ten animals, known as packs. All breeds of domestic dogs, large or small, are descended from the gray wolf.

VERTEBRATES

Most **wolf packs** are family groups. They are led by an "alpha" wolf that has fought fellow family members to become the leader of the pack.

Wolves howl to call their pack together and to communicate across long distances.

A FLYING VISIT

Not all birds can live for as long as an albatross, which might make it to 40 years. Many are here for just five to ten years, including the eastern bluebird and the Carolina wren. Other species also live for such a short amount of time, it's a fleeting visit.

7–8 years The **small crested auklet** lives in large colonies of more than a million birds. In the breeding season, this seabird produces an orangey perfume to try to attract a mate.

6–10 years The male **eastern bluebird** attracts females by singing, flapping its wings, and gathering nesting materials. It is fiercely territorial and attacks any other birds that might compete for food.

MICROORGANISMS
PLANTS AND FUNGI
INVERTEBRATES
VERTEBRATES

7 years The aquatic **pink sea squirt** has two openings in its body: one to suck in water and food, and the other to squirt out waste. When disturbed, it squirts jets of fluid at anything in its way.

6–7 years The claws of the **Florida stone crab** are harvested by fishermen in Florida, where they are considered a delicacy. Only the claw is taken, and the live crab is returned to the water. Within a few months the crab will grow a whole new claw.

HOW STRONG IS A CRAB'S CLAW?

The stone crab's claws can exert a crushing force of over 120,000 lb. per square inch (9,000kg per square centimeter). That's 93 times more than the jaws of an average human.

6–10 years The empty "tests," or shells, of the **common sand dollar** often wash up on beaches. Scientists can tell the age of a sand dollar by counting the rings on its test.

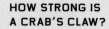

I MONTH   I YEAR   2 YEARS   5 YEARS   IO YEARS   20 YEARS   30 YEARS   50 YEARS

6 years The **white-tailed deer** avoids predators by gathering and swallowing its food very quickly, before moving on to a safer place. Once there, it spits the food back up into its mouth in order to chew it. It then digests this food in a series of four different stomachs.

6 years **Carolina wrens** are fiercely territorial. Once a male has found a mate, the pair stay together for life. Severe winters in Canada and the northern United States are threatening wren populations there.

RAISING THE ALARM

When a white-tailed deer detects a possible predator, it raises its tail to reveal its white bottom. This is a silent way of telling the rest of the herd that danger is close by.

7 years Before going to sleep, **parrotfish** produce a layer of mucus that covers their body. Scientists believe that this protective slime helps hide their scent from predators.

7 years All orange **clown fish** are born male. When a female dies, a male in the group changes sex and becomes a female. Once a male has changed to a female, it can never change back.

HUMMINGBIRDS

A hummingbird's wings can beat up to 200 times per second, making a humming noise, while its heart rate can be as high as 1,260 beats per minute. In order to find the energy to do this, hummingbirds drink 200 percent of their own body weight in sugars every day. In addition to drinking nectar, an estimated five to ten percent of a hummingbird's daily diet consists of tiny arthropods, such as spiders and insects, for protein. Despite their frenetic activity, most hummingbirds live for around seven years.

VERTEBRATES

Flying backward is a skill that is unique to hummingbirds.

*The male bee hummingbird is the **world's smallest bird**, at just 2 in. (5cm) long.*

| I MONTH | I YEAR | 2 YEARS | 5 YEARS | IO YEARS | 20 YEARS | 30 YEARS | 50 YEARS |

Ruby-throated hummingbird

DO YOU MIND IF I JOIN YOU?

Some species are parasites, which means that they do not fend for themselves. Instead, they attach to other organisms, called hosts, and steal shelter, food, and resources. While the parasites benefit from this lazy lifestyle, their hosts will suffer and may even die.

Ascaris lumbricoides is a parasitic nematode, or roundworm, that lives in the intestines of humans (*illustration right*), causing a disease called ascariasis. As many as 1.2 billion people all over the world are infected with *Ascaris*, though few have any symptoms.

1 *Microscopic* Ascaris *eggs on food, animal, or household objects are ingested (swallowed) by a human host.*

8 *Days 75–100: sticky, infectious eggs get caught under human fingernails and eaten by accident. Others are transferred onto food and everyday objects by carriers such as flies, cockroaches, and dogs. Dogs can become hosts to* Ascaris *worms, too.*

7 *Days 55–75: the eggs are passed in feces (poop). Over the next three weeks, eggs develop and spread on the poop in warm, moist conditions.*

lungs

stomach

small intestine

Purple martin birds play host to an unusually high number of parasites. Blowflies lay eggs in the birds' nests, fleas feed on their blood, and lice bite off pieces of their skin.

It is best not to urinate (pee) while wading in the Amazon River. The tiny **candirú**, or toothpick fish, has been known to swim up a flow of urine and lodge itself inside the human body.

Sea lampreys use their razor-sharp teeth and suction-cup mouths to attach themselves to sharks and other fish, feeding on their blood and tissue. They have also been known to attack humans, clamping onto the backs of swimmers.

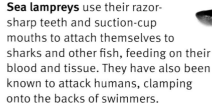

The **corpse flower** has no leaves, roots, or shoots and is invisible until it blooms to produce the world's largest flower, at up to 3 ft. (1m) across. It steals nutrients and water from its grapevine host and sends out a smell like rotting flesh to attract pollinating insects.

2 *Day 1:* eggs hatch into larvae inside the small intestine.

3 *Days 1–2:* larvae migrate through the intestinal wall.

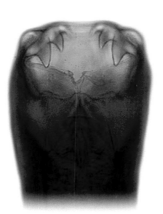

Don't walk barefoot in the tropics—**hookworm** larvae might chew their way into your feet. Hookworms can live for many months or years in the small intestines of humans.

4 *Days 5–6:* larvae are carried up to the lungs, where they mature.

Schistosoma are tiny parasitic worms that live inside freshwater snails (*right*). They cause a disease in humans called schistosomiasis, or bilharzia, which seriously damages internal organs. More than 200 million people are infected worldwide.

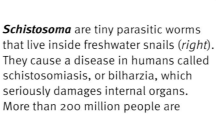

5 *Days 10–14:* mature larvae are coughed up and swallowed, entering the small intestine again.

6 *Ascaris* worms can live for two to three years in the small intestine. Each worm can grow to 14 in. (35cm) long.

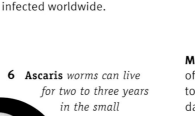

Mistletoe plants grow on the branches of trees and steal water and minerals to grow. Although their presence is damaging for the host tree, many birds depend on mistletoe for food and shelter.

6 *Days 50–55:* mature larvae develop into adult worms, and then mate. A female worm can lay as many as 200,000 eggs per day.

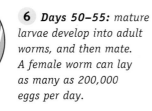

Head lice, or nits, live and reproduce on human heads, cementing their eggs (*below*) onto hair. Baby lice hatch after seven to ten days and feed by sucking blood through the scalp.

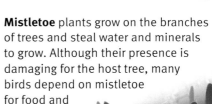

DON'T STOP ME NOW!

Some species give off elaborate warnings to tell everyone that they are dangerous and should be left alone. Many of these species, such as the golden poison-arrow frog, really are lethal and will kill in self-defense. Others, such as the frill-necked lizard, are actually harmless and are bluffing in the hope that they will live a little longer.

5–10 years The **golden poison-arrow frog** is the world's most poisonous animal. Its skin is covered in a toxin so lethal that just 4 oz. (1g) could kill at least 10,000 humans. The Embera Chocó people of Colombia carefully extract the poison and use it to tip their arrows.

5–8 years In the game of ferret "legging," the winner is the person who lasts the longest with a sharp-toothed **ferret** down their pants. Originally from Great Britain, the game is now played in the state of Virginia.

MICROORGANISMS
PLANTS AND FUNGI
INVERTEBRATES
VERTEBRATES

5–10 years When frightened, the **frill-necked lizard** unfurls its frill and hisses confidently. If that fails to scare off a predator, the terrified lizard will run away.

5–7 years Humans have kept **chickens** for thousands of years, as pets and for eggs and meat. Today, there are thought to be 17 billion chickens in the world—that's 2.5 chickens for every person.

OFFICER, I'VE LOST MY PIRANHA!

It is illegal to own a piranha in many countries, in case it escapes and eats native animals.

7–9 years **Red-bellied piranhas** have razor-sharp teeth. They use these to strip the flesh from prey. Despite their fearsome reputation, their diet consists mainly of small fish and insects.

| 1 MONTH | 1 YEAR | 2 YEARS | 5 YEARS | 10 YEARS | 20 YEARS | 30 YEARS | 50 YEARS |

7–10 years **Giant African millipedes** can grow as long as 15.2 in. (38.7cm) and have up to 256 legs. They secrete an irritating liquid that helps frighten off predators.

10 years **Raspberry** plants produce sweet red fruit that are ready to pick in the summer. Their leaves are also used to make traditional medicines that treat problems with the digestive system.

5–10 years **Snowy owls** live mostly in the arctic, preying on small mammals such as the meadow vole. Owls swallow their prey whole and digest its flesh, before regurgitating (vomiting up) the bones, teeth, and fur.

5–8 years Poisonous **puffers**, or blowfish, are a delicacy in Japan, but dining on one is dicing with death. If your chef fails to prepare it properly, you could be dead before dinner is over.

9 years **Vampire bats** hunt at night, preying on humans and other mammals. They bite into their victim with razor-sharp teeth, and then lap up blood from the wound. They urinate (pee) while drinking to make room for even more blood.

6–8 years Female **Tasmanian devils** give birth to up to 40 young, each the size of a grain of rice. Despite this, the mother produces only enough milk for four baby devils to survive.

75 YEARS **100 YEARS** **200 YEARS** **500 YEARS** **1,000 YEARS** **5,000 YEARS**

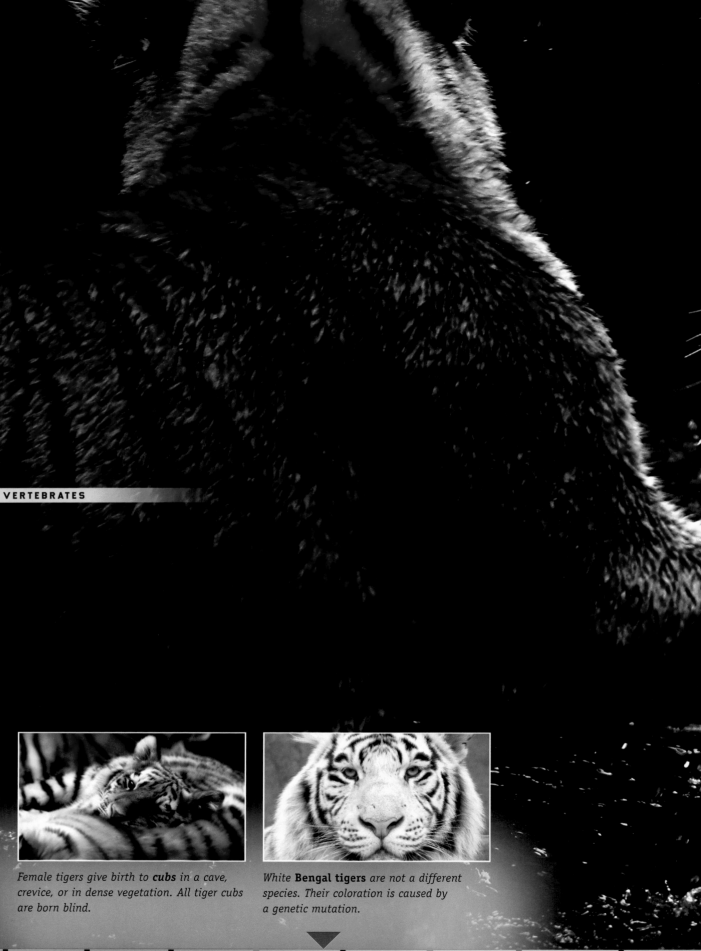

VERTEBRATES

Female tigers give birth to **cubs** in a cave, crevice, or in dense vegetation. All tiger cubs are born blind.

White **Bengal tigers** are not a different species. Their coloration is caused by a genetic mutation.

| I MONTH | I YEAR | 2 YEARS | 5 YEARS | IO YEARS | 20 YEARS | 30 YEARS | 50 YEARS |

TIGERS

The magnificent Amur tiger lives in the forests of eastern Russia, in an area known as Siberia. Despite being the largest and heaviest of all cats, these tigers are no match for people: we humans have hunted Amur tigers close to extinction, and only 450 are now left in the wild. Ninety-seven percent of all wild tigers have died out over the last 100 years, largely due to poaching and habitat loss.

75 YEARS | **100** YEARS | **200** YEARS | **500** YEARS | **1,000** YEARS | **5,000** YEARS

The **castor oil plant** is the most poisonous plant in the world. It produces castor beans, which contain a deadly chemical called ricin. If the beans are chewed and swallowed, they can kill a person within hours.

Annual plants live for one year, and biennials live for two. Many plants, such as this peony, live for much longer and have no definite life span. These plants are called **perennials**. If they get enough water and sunlight, they continue to grow year after year.

The stomach of a **glass frog** is covered in translucent, or almost see-through, skin. The frog's internal organs, such as its heart and intestines, are visible from outside of its body.

The **common basilisk** is found in the tropical rainforests of Central and South America. Large, flat feet allow these lizards to run across the surface of lakes and ponds. After several feet, they sink and are forced to swim.

In 2005, the Australian government sent four **Tasmanian devils** to Denmark as a wedding gift to Crown Prince Frederik and his Tasmanian bride, Mary. These devils are the only living ones that can be seen outside Australia. Because they are highly endangered, devils are never normally allowed to leave the country.

10-50 YEARS

SEEING DOUBLE

All of these species have made it to ten years old, and their age is in double digits. None of them will make it to triple figures, as none will live to be 100. Some might live to see their 20th year, but for now, ten years is a life well lived.

11 years The African **black mamba** is the fastest snake in the world, able to move at up to 15 mph (24km/h). Black mambas attack their prey viciously, striking several times. Their powerful venom can kill a human in just 20 minutes.

ARE BLACK MAMBAS BLACK?

No, they are actually green. "Black" mamba refers to the black coloration inside the mamba's mouth, which frightens off predators.

MICROORGANISMS
PLANTS AND FUNGI
INVERTEBRATES
VERTEBRATES

12 years **Hoffman's two-toed sloths** are incredibly sluggish, spending almost all of their time in trees, hanging upside down. Sloths always come down to the ground to defecate, or poop, as the sound of their feces falling from a tree could attract predators. To avoid going to the ground very often, lazy sloths poop just once a week.

12–15 years The armored **nine-banded armadillo** can jump up to 4 ft. (1.2m) when frightened. Mothers always give birth to four identical young.

15 years **Mexican axolotls** can only be found in Lake Xochimilco in Mexico. Unfortunately, this lake is polluted and drying up, threatening these delicate amphibians.

I MONTH | I YEAR | 2 YEARS | 5 YEARS | IO YEARS | 20 YEARS | 30 YEARS | 50 YEARS

13 years

The **blue land crab** is found along the Atlantic coast of the Americas. It is a terrestrial animal, which means that it lives on land. Sometimes these crabs are cannibals, eating each other for food.

13 years

The **caecilian** is a wormlike amphibian. The offspring survive by eating their mother's skin, which they scrape away using needlelike teeth.

16 years

Cheetahs are the fastest animals on land. They can run at 75 mph (120km/h), and can accelerate from 0–60 mph (0–97km/h) in under three seconds—much faster than a racing car. Despite these extraordinary talents, their life span is similar to that of a domestic cat.

12–14 years

Meerkats are small mammals that live in groups of around 20 individuals. Some meerkats stand upright and keep watch for enemies. If a predator is spotted, they "bark" to warn the rest of the group, who then run to the safety of their underground tunnels.

SEA COW OR MERMAID?

Some people say manatees are called sea cows because, like cows, they are vegetarians. Others say it is because they taste like beef. Historians believe that when sailors claimed to have spotted mermaids, they had, in fact, seen manatees.

12 years

The aquatic **Amazonian manatee** is also known as a sea cow. It can keep replacing its old teeth, which have been ground down by grazing plants on the seabed, with new ones throughout its life. This is unique among mammals.

75 YEARS | **100 YEARS** | **200 YEARS** | **500 YEARS** | **1,000 YEARS** | **5,000 YEARS**

VERTEBRATES

1 MONTH 1 YEAR 2 YEARS 5 YEARS 10 YEARS 20 YEARS 30 YEARS 50 YEARS

DOGS

Dogs are the domesticated, or tamed, relatives of wild gray wolves. Unlike their vicious ancestors, dogs are often thought of as man's best friend and are widely kept as pets—in the United States alone, almost 40 percent of households have a dog in the family. Although dogs are all the same species, their appearance varies greatly. Each breed has a different name, and mixed-breed dogs are called mongrels.

Assistance dogs *are specially trained to help humans. This Saint Bernard can help in mountain rescue operations.*

Many pet dogs, like this cocker spaniel, are *treated as one of the family* *and have many toys and possessions.*

NOT JUST A PRETTY FACE

Most animals need to find a mate before they can have any offspring. For some species, including sheep, any mate will do—but for others, such as birds of paradise, choosing a partner is not such a simple affair . . .

12–18 years **Rocky Mountain goats** live in freezing temperatures at the very tops of mountains. Males stab each other with their sharp horns to fight for the attention of female goats.

10–12 years **Sheep** are intelligent animals that can learn their own names and recognize faces. Some intelligent sheep have learned to cross cattle grids by rolling over them on their backs.

MICROORGANISMS
PLANTS AND FUNGI
INVERTEBRATES
VERTEBRATES

11 years **Wild boar** are found across much of the world, as far south as Indonesia. Males use their sharp tusks to fight off rivals during the breeding season.

LET THE SUN SHINE IN!
Reindeer are the only mammals that can see ultraviolet light, which causes sunburn.

15 years **Caribou**, or reindeer, live in and around the Arctic. Males and females both grow antlers, which shed, or fall off, each year. Brand new ones then grow in their place.

12–13 years Male **birds of paradise** (*below*) must perform an elaborate dance in order to win a female's affections. This complex performance can last for many hours.

15–20 years **Toucans** (*left*) are found in South America and are famous for their big, bright bills. These act like radiators—they store or release heat, helping the birds to stay warm or cool down. The bill is filled with air pockets to stop it from being too heavy.

11–12 years **Common marmosets** are native to the forests of Brazil. As well as eating plants and insects, these monkeys feed on tree sap. Marmosets often give birth to two fraternal, or nonidentical, twins.

13–14 years **Tarsiers**, or bush babies, are nocturnal, meaning that they sleep during the day and are only active at night. Their huge eyes help them see in the dark. Although tarsiers were once found all over the world, today they are only found in Southeast Asia.

14 years **Giant anteaters** can stick out their tongues more than 160 times per minute, licking up as many as 35,000 ants or termites per day.

VERTEBRATES

Lazy lions **rest for up to 20 hours** per day. They are most active at night, when it is much cooler.

Female lions, or lionesses, are **more athletic than males** and do most of the hunting to feed their cubs.

| 1 MONTH | 1 YEAR | 2 YEARS | 5 YEARS | 10 YEARS | 20 YEARS | 30 YEARS | 50 YEARS |

LIONS

Lions live in groups, called prides, of up to 40 animals. Most members of the pride are females and their offspring, with only one to three males in a group. Although female lions might live to be 15 years old, male lions rarely reach the age of ten. Their life spans are cut short by dangerous fights with other males as they battle to protect their pride.

75 YEARS | 100 YEARS | 200 YEARS | 500 YEARS | 1,000 YEARS | 5,000 YEARS

CONFUSING CREATURES

Why does the periodical cicada wait for 17 years to die, and why does the venomous platypus have a duck's bill and a beaver's tail? We have learned a lot in recent years about the organisms that share our planet, but some species still puzzle us today.

WHAT ARE MONOTREMES?

Monotremes are mammals that lay eggs instead of giving birth to live young.

11–17 years **Platypuses** are monotremes that live in eastern Australia. When threatened, males stab their enemies with special spurs, or spikes, on their back feet. These inject a cocktail of venom that is strong enough to kill a small dog.

MICROORGANISMS
PLANTS AND FUNGI
INVERTEBRATES
VERTEBRATES

10 years Most penguins avoid climbing over obstacles and choose to slide around them. Tough **rockhopper penguins** prefer a more adventurous approach. They jump over rocks and boulders to get to the other side.

WHERE DO PENGUINS LIVE?

Penguins don't just live in Antarctica. They are also found in South America, South Africa, Australia, and New Zealand.

15–16 years The **largemouth bass** is a freshwater fish found across North America. This bass is the official fish of four states: Alabama, Florida, Georgia, and Mississippi.

| I MONTH | I YEAR | 2 YEARS | 5 YEARS | IO YEARS | 20 YEARS | 30 YEARS | 50 YEARS |

17 years **Periodical cicadas** start life as tiny nymphs that feed on plant roots underground. After 17 years they burrow to the surface, mature into adults, lay eggs, and die after just a few weeks.

15 years Fewer than 2,500 **giant pandas** are left in the mountains of China. Deforestation and habitat loss are pushing these bears to extinction.

20 years Male **mandrills** have brightly colored faces that help warn others that they are in charge. Older and more dominant mandrills have brighter faces than other males.

18–20 years **Mantas** can grow up to 23 ft. (7m) wide and weigh more than 2,860 lb. (1,300kg)—about the same as a small walrus. They need to swim constantly to stop their heavy bodies from sinking.

17 years **Koalas** are among very few mammals with fingerprints. Their prints are so similar to human ones that it is difficult to tell them apart.

SNAKES

Almost 3,000 species of snakes can be found across the world, on every continent except Antarctica. Snakes are among the most feared of all animals on Earth—bites from venomous species kill several thousand people each year. Despite this, most snakes are nonvenomous and are not able to kill with a bite. Instead, they coil tightly around their prey and slowly crush it to death.

VERTEBRATES

Viper snake

| I MONTH | I YEAR | 2 YEARS | 5 YEARS | IO YEARS | 20 YEARS | 30 YEARS | 50 YEARS |

The Mozambique spitting cobra can **spray venom** for up to 10 ft. (3m), blinding anything in its path.

Some snakes, such as this Arizona mountain king snake, regularly kill and **eat other species of snake**.

TIME FLIES WHEN YOU'RE HAVING FUN

Life is tough for peacocks, whose colorful tails make them easy for predators to catch. Surviving is simpler for other animals. Bald eagles and polar bears, for example, are at the top of the food chain and have no natural predators to flee from.

Atlantic puffins spend most of their lives at sea. They only return to land in the spring and summer to build nests and raise baby pufflings.

20 years

HOW DO PUFFINS FIND FOOD?

Puffins are excellent swimmers and can dive to depths of 200 ft. (60m) in search of fish to eat.

MICROORGANISMS
PLANTS AND FUNGI
INVERTEBRATES
VERTEBRATES

15–25 years

The **Japanese flowering cherry** is found across the Far East. Its pretty flowers, called cherry blossoms, bloom each spring and are very important in Japanese culture. Thousands of people gather each year to relax and celebrate under the flowering trees.

20 years

Indian peacocks have elaborate tails that make them attractive to females (peahens). Their beauty comes at a price, however: large, colorful tails are much easier for predators to snatch.

| I MONTH | I YEAR | 2 YEARS | 5 YEARS | IO YEARS | 2O YEARS | 3O YEARS | 5O YEARS |

28–30 years — **Bald eagle** pairs mate for life. Together, they build a giant nest in which they raise up to three offspring per year. The biggest nest ever recorded weighed 2 tons (1.81 metric tonnes)—even more than a hippopotamus.

20–24 years — **Beavers** have sharp teeth to cut down trees, which they use to build "dams" in rivers. These dams divert water and create tranquil lakes for the beavers to live in.

20–30 years — **European herring gulls** (*left*) often steal food from passing people. When gulls feel threatened, they spray their enemies with feces (poop) and vomit.

20–29 years — A single female **Atlantic cod** (*left*) can produce nine million eggs in a single year. Despite this, cod populations are rapidly declining due to overfishing by humans.

25–30 years — **Polar bears** are the largest land-living carnivores, or meat eaters, on Earth. Despite their white appearance, their skin is black and their hair is completely transparent.

27–30 years — **Atlantic blue marlins** use their swordlike bills to slash their way through schools of fish. They soar through the water at up to 60 mph (96km/h), then swim back to feed on injured fish.

75 YEARS   **100 YEARS**   **200 YEARS**   **500 YEARS**   **1,000 YEARS**   **5,000 YEARS**

HORSES

Humans have domesticated horses over many thousands of years. In the past, they were used to pull chariots and haul heavy machinery. Today, we race them for sport, ride them for fun, and even train them to help in the police force. The height of a horse is measured in hands. One hand equals 4 in. (10.16cm). Horses less than 14.2 hands (56.8 in./144.27cm) are called ponies.

VERTEBRATES

| 1 MONTH | 1 YEAR | 2 YEARS | 5 YEARS | 10 YEARS | 20 YEARS | 30 YEARS | 50 YEARS |

Shetland ponies come from islands off the northeast coast of Scotland. **Thick winter fur** helps them keep warm in the cold.

The **only wild horse**, Przewalski's horse, was once extinct outside of zoos. It has since been reintroduced into Central Asia.

20–30 YEARS

NOW YOU SEE ME . . .

. . . now you don't. Many species have special coloration, called camouflage, which helps them hide from predators. Red kangaroos blend in with sandy deserts, while zebras' black-and-white stripes help them confuse hungry predators.

POOP POWER

In the Andes Mountains, local people burn llama feces (poop) for fuel.

15–28
years

Llamas live in South America and are closely related to camels. When angry, they rear up on their hind legs and spit the contents of their stomach all over their enemies.

MICROORGANISMS
PLANTS AND FUNGI
INVERTEBRATES
VERTEBRATES

20–25
years

Highland cattle come from western Scotland and are one of the oldest breeds of cattle. They have a thick mop of hair on their heads to protect their eyes from wind and rain. This helps them cope in the cold Scottish climate.

16–25
years

Red kangaroos are marsupials and so give birth to undeveloped offspring. Joeys, or infants, are born after 33 days and must develop for another six months in a pouch on their mother's stomach.

1 MONTH	**1 YEAR**	**2 YEARS**	**5 YEARS**	**10 YEARS**	**20 YEARS**	**30 YEARS**	**50 YEARS**

25 years Many people think that the **plains zebra** has white skin with black stripes. In fact, it is the other way around: their skin is black, and their stripes are white.

28 years **Naked mole rats** are the world's longest-living rodents and are completely immune to cancer. Scientists are studying their DNA to try and figure out why they live for so long.

25–30 years **Malayan tapirs** live in Southeast Asia. Although much of their body is black, they have a bold white stripe across their backs. This acts as a type of camouflage, helping them hide from tigers and other predators.

ARE OKAPI RELATED TO ZEBRAS?

Despite their black-and-white stripes, okapi are close cousins of giraffes, not zebras.

20–30 years **Okapi** live in the rainforests of Central Africa and are very shy animals. Until 1901, scientists had no proof that okapi even existed.

20-30 years During the summer, **grizzly bears** put on 440 lb. (200kg) in weight —the equivalent of two large men. This extra fat helps them survive the winter months.

SHARKS

Sharks can smell one drop of blood in a million drops of water and use their razor-sharp teeth to rip their prey into meaty chunks. Sharks rarely attack humans, but they have been known to do so when hungry or provoked. When the warship *U.S.S. Indianapolis* sank in 1945, almost 900 sailors were left in shark-infested waters. By the time help arrived four days later, only 316 had survived attacks from sharks.

VERTEBRATES

*Tiger sharks are extremely aggressive. They frequently **attack inedible objects** and have even tried to eat sunken cars.*

*The wide head of a hammerhead shark **enhances its vision**, allowing the shark to see above and below at the same time.*

| 1 MONTH | 1 YEAR | 2 YEARS | 5 YEARS | 10 YEARS | 20 YEARS | 30 YEARS | 50 YEARS |

Great white shark

75 YEARS | 100 YEARS | 200 YEARS | 500 YEARS | 1,000 YEARS | 5,000 YEARS

I'M STICKING WITH YOU

Sometimes, we like to do things by ourselves—but often it is nice to have someone to help. Many different species work together in order to make life easier. Instead of working alone, they get by with a little help from their friends.

1 *Acacia trees give **white-backed vultures** a place to shelter and reproduce. Vultures can look out from the tops of the trees and survey the savanna for food.*

Acacia trees, or thorn trees (*right*), are found all over the world. They commonly grow in the African savanna, where they form special partnerships with other species.

Pea plants work closely with microorganisms called rhizobia. These bacteria live in the soil and swap nutrients with the plants, which helps both species survive.

2 *Leopards drag the heavy bodies of their prey to the branches of trees for safe keeping. This stops rivals from stealing their food.*

3 *Red-billed oxpeckers sit on many large mammals, such as this impala, and eat ticks off their skin. The oxpeckers never go hungry, and the impalas are parasite-free.*

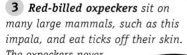

Remora fish are too lazy to swim for themselves. Instead, they attach themselves to unsuspecting sharks and hold on tight for the ride.

8 *The East African whistling thorn acacia works closely with* **cocktail ants**. *The ants help the tree by fiercely biting any animals that try to eat its leaves. In return, they live in swollen thorns and eat nectar from the branches of the tree.*

Bees drink nectar from the plants that they visit. While there, they transfer pollen from the male part of the flower (the anther) to the female part (the stigma). Once this happens, the plant can reproduce.

7 *Some plant leaves, including the acacia, contain a natural medicine that helps kill parasites in* **chimpanzees**. *The plant's seeds are then released in the chimpanzee's feces and grow into brand-new plants.*

5 *Snakes shelter in the branches of trees and wait to snatch birds from their nests or to drop down on prey.*

6 *Giraffes play host to millions of bacteria that live inside their stomachs. In exchange for shelter, these bacteria help giraffes digest the acacia tree's tough leaves.*

Hungry **clown fish** protect venomous sea anemones by killing and eating their predators. In return, the fish live and breed inside the anemones' arms and are not affected by their venom.

4 *Acacias are much healthier when they grow next to* **termite mounds**. *Termites recycle the soil and make it nutrient-rich, which helps the trees grow.*

Ratels, or honey badgers, find beehives with the help of greater honeyguide birds. They then rip open the hives and eat the honey, but leave the bee larvae as food for the birds.

ALL IN GOOD TIME

Different species live life at different paces. Some, such as the ostrich, can race around the savanna at 40 mph (65km/h). Others, like the walrus, weigh up to 3,750 lb. (1,700kg)—about the same as a medium-size car. With so much weight to carry, they would rather not hurry around.

25–35 years — Baby **harp seals**, called pups, are born with fluffy white coats. These coats turn gray after just three weeks.

35–40 years — The **Pacific walrus** uses its ivory tusks to break through ice while swimming. These tusks can grow to be up to 3 ft. (1m) in length.

MICROORGANISMS
PLANTS AND FUNGI
INVERTEBRATES
VERTEBRATES

30–40 years — **Bonobos** are very similar to chimpanzees but are actually a different species. They are very social animals and form strong bonds with each other.

30–40 years — The **wandering albatross** has the greatest wingspan of any bird—as wide as 11 ft. (3.5m). It can fly for several thousands of miles nonstop in search of food.

I MONTH | I YEAR | 2 YEARS | 5 YEARS | IO YEARS | 20 YEARS | 30 YEARS | 50 YEARS

WHAT ARE RHINO HORNS MADE OF?

Rhino horns are made entirely of thickly matted hair called keratin. This is the same material that makes up human hair and fingernails.

40–50 years Poachers have hunted the **white rhino** to near-extinction for its horns. These horns are carved into statues and sculptures or are used in traditional medicines.

40–50 years **Hippopotamuses** defecate (poop) to mark their territories and swing their tails around to bat their poop across wider areas. They also urinate backward, spraying anyone who might be behind them.

40–50 years When thirsty, **dromedary camels** can drink up to 26 gal. (100l) of water in one go. Humans can just about manage 0.5 gal. (2l).

30–50 years **Ostrich** are the biggest birds in the world. A single ostrich eyeball is larger than its brain. Its egg—the biggest of any bird—can weigh up to 5.7 lb. (2.59kg), which is more than 45 times heavier than a chicken's egg.

75 YEARS   **100 YEARS**   **200 YEARS**   **500 YEARS**   **1,000 YEARS**   **5,000 YEARS**

GREAT APES

Orangutans live in Southeast Asia and are among the most intelligent of animals. They can use tools, "speak" in sign language, and solve complex problems. It is not surprising that they are so similar to us—orangutans, chimpanzees, gorillas, and bonobos are our closest living relatives on Earth, and up to 98.7 percent of our DNA is the same. Together, we are called the "great apes."

VERTEBRATES

*In some regions of Africa, chimpanzees have **learned to use stone tools** to crack open tasty oil-palm nuts.*

*Instead of walking upright, gorillas often **walk on their knuckles**. A dominant silverback male is always in charge.*

| I MONTH | I YEAR | 2 YEARS | 5 YEARS | IO YEARS | 20 YEARS | 30 YEARS | 50 YEARS |

ANYTHING YOU CAN DO . . .

. . . they can do better. If you think that humans are talented, you should see what some other animals can do. Every species has its own special skill that separates it from the crowd. Beluga whales can swim backward, sifakas show off their dance moves, and the stench of a titan arum is so disgusting that it might even make you throw up.

HOW DO FEMALE HORNBILLS EAT?

Females rely on male hornbills to feed them and their offspring, through a small slit in the door of their nest.

30–35 years For protection, female **rhinoceros hornbills** raise their offspring in holes in tree trunks. They seal themselves inside by building a door made mostly of feces, or poop.

MICROORGANISMS
PLANTS AND FUNGI
INVERTEBRATES
VERTEBRATES

30–35 years **Sifakas** are a type of lemur that live in Madagascar. They move by leaping around on two legs, which makes them look like they are dancing. Scientists are not sure how long sifakas live, but some studies suggest that females might survive into their 30s.

30–50 years **Komodo dragon** saliva is very toxic: it contains a powerful venom and deadly bacteria. Dragons bite their prey and then wait patiently for their saliva to kill it.

| MONTH | I YEAR | 2 YEARS | 5 YEARS | IO YEARS | 20 YEARS | 30 YEARS | 50 YEARS |

40–50 years Although most animals breathe without thinking, **bottle-nosed dolphins** must constantly remember to breathe. To stop them from drowning, only one half of their brain goes to sleep at a time.

40–50 years **Cassowaries** live in New Guinea and Australia. Despite their frugivorous, or fruit-eating, nature, these birds are capable of attacking and killing their enemies. Their feet have sharp, daggerlike claws that can easily rip open a human.

40–50 years The **titan arum** grows in the rainforests of western Sumatra. It smells like a rotting animal, which helps attract pollinators such as beetles and flies. For this reason, it is often called the "corpse flower."

SUPER STINKER!
The tallest ever titan arum grew to a height of 10.2 ft. (3.1m). That's about as tall as an elephant.

35–50 years Unlike most other whales, **beluga whales** can swim backward. This helps them navigate through Arctic ice. Baby belugas are born gray and turn white as they grow older.

30–50 years Tiny **kiwis** are only found in New Zealand. Their range is very restricted because they cannot fly. Despite their small size, female kiwis lay giant eggs that are six times bigger than a chicken's egg.

75 YEARS | **100 YEARS** | **200 YEARS** | **500 YEARS** | **1,000 YEARS** | **5,000 YEARS**

WHALES

Whales live in the depths of every ocean on Earth, but are often seen breaching, or jumping, out of the water. Scientists are not sure why this happens, but it is thought that they might breach to communicate with others. Some whale species, such as this humpback whale, also communicate by singing special "songs." These melodies are similar to man-made music and help whales attract a mate.

VERTEBRATES

Female **killer whales,** or orcas, can live for 90 years. Males live much shorter lives, surviving for little more than 30 years.

Because whales are mammals, they cannot breathe underwater. Instead, they breathe through **blowholes** on the top of their head.

| I MONTH | I YEAR | 2 YEARS | 5 YEARS | IO YEARS | 20 YEARS | 30 YEARS | 50 YEARS |

Humpback whale

?

Unlike those of most other mammals, **kangaroo** farts do not pollute the environment. Special bacteria in their stomachs convert damaging methane gases into harmless liquids, which cannot damage the ozone layer. Scientists plan to put these bacteria inside the stomachs of cows, whose constant methane farting is speeding up global warming.

Gorillas are the largest animals that build nests to sleep in. They construct comfortable mattresses from branches and leaves. Most gorilla nests are built on the ground, but some, such as this one, are made high up in the trees.

Dromedary camels are naturally found across Africa and the Middle East. In the 1800s, a small number were introduced to Australia to help transport people and goods. Since then, they have reproduced so much that more than a million camels now roam free in the country.

Hippopotamuses have mucus glands in their skin that produce a gloopy, bright-red liquid. This fluid hardens into a natural sunscreen, which stops the hippos from burning in the sun.

You can tell the age of a **walrus** by looking at the growth rings on the inside of its tusks. Older walrus have more rings than younger ones.

LONG-DISTANCE RUNNERS

50-100 YEARS

FINALLY FIFTY

After living for half a century, these species have something to celebrate. Fifty years on Earth is quite an achievement—individuals of many other species died off years ago. If these organisms are not too old to party, it might be time for another cake . . .

**MICROORGANISMS
PLANTS AND FUNGI
INVERTEBRATES
VERTEBRATES**

| 50 years | The **golden weeping willow** tree originally came from Asia. It is famous for its drooping branches, which make it look as though the tree is crying. |

| 50 years | **American flamingos** are colored by their diet. They snack on small crustaceans that contain chemicals called carotenoids. These turn the flamingos' feathers bright pink. |

YOU ARE WHAT YOU EAT!

Zookeepers feed flamingos an artificial source of carotenoids, to make certain that they turn pink.

| 50 years | The **alligator gar** is the largest freshwater fish in North America. Females lay highly poisonous eggs as a way to stop predators from eating them. Although females can live for more than 50 years, males rarely live past their 25th birthday. |

| I MONTH | I YEAR | 2 YEARS | 5 YEARS | 10 YEARS | 20 YEARS | 30 YEARS | 50 YEARS |

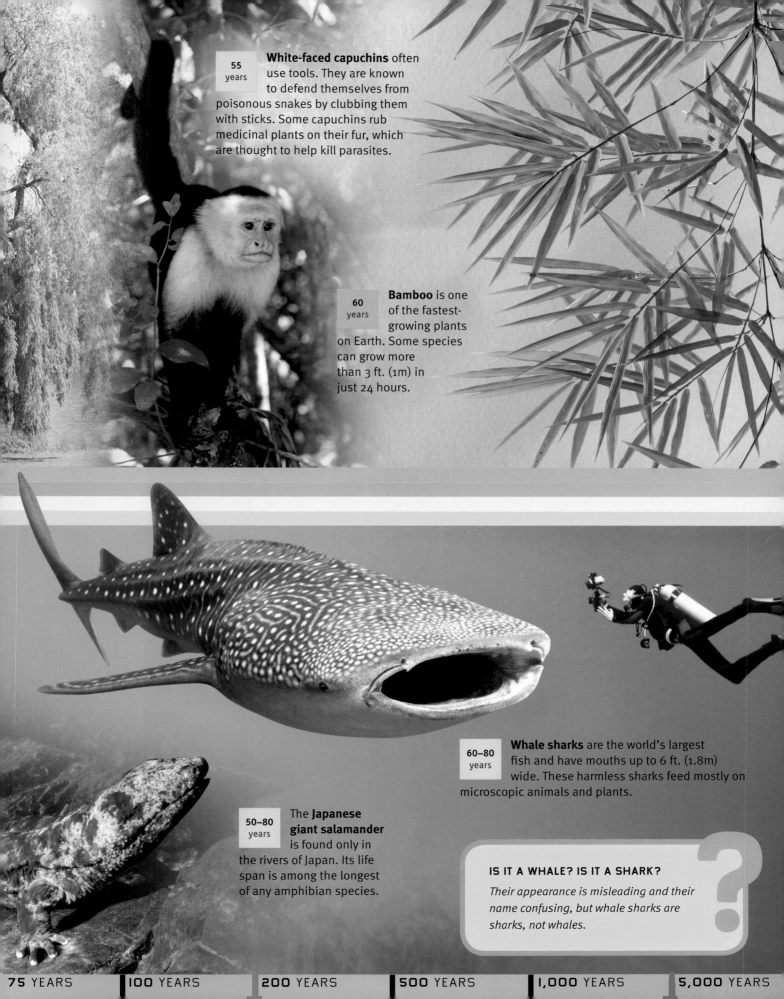

55 years **White-faced capuchins** often use tools. They are known to defend themselves from poisonous snakes by clubbing them with sticks. Some capuchins rub medicinal plants on their fur, which are thought to help kill parasites.

60 years **Bamboo** is one of the fastest-growing plants on Earth. Some species can grow more than 3 ft. (1m) in just 24 hours.

60–80 years **Whale sharks** are the world's largest fish and have mouths up to 6 ft. (1.8m) wide. These harmless sharks feed mostly on microscopic animals and plants.

50–80 years The **Japanese giant salamander** is found only in the rivers of Japan. Its life span is among the longest of any amphibian species.

IS IT A WHALE? IS IT A SHARK?

Their appearance is misleading and their name confusing, but whale sharks are sharks, not whales.

ELEPHANTS

Elephants can be found in the forests and savannas of Africa and Asia. They are the largest land animals on Earth. Although most weigh around 11,000 lb. (5,000kg), the heaviest elephant on record weighed 24,000 lb. (10,886kg)— more than seven average cars. Female elephants, or cows, live in social groups called herds, while male elephants, called bulls, live alone.

VERTEBRATES

| I MONTH | I YEAR | 2 YEARS | 5 YEARS | IO YEARS | 20 YEARS | 30 YEARS | 50 YEARS |

*Elephants suck water into their **powerful trunks** and spray it on their backs to cool down. Their trunks contain 40,000 muscles.*

*Poachers still kill elephants for their **ivory tusks**, even though it is illegal. Ivory is carved into expensive ornaments and jewelry.*

GUESS MY AGE

We can determine the life span of an individual by watching it closely, from birth until death. Some species, like cockatoos, can be kept as pets and their ages are easy to record. Others, such as the dugong, live freely in the oceans and are more difficult for us to keep track of.

60–80 years It can take up to 80 years for the gigantic **talipot palm** to flower. Shortly after doing so, the palm tree produces fruit and dies.

MICROORGANISMS
PLANTS AND FUNGI
INVERTEBRATES
VERTEBRATES

50–70 years **Dugongs** can hold their breath for six minutes underwater before they need to swim to the surface for air. They live in warm coastal waters from Africa to Australia and are closely related to manatees.

FLOWER POWER

The talipot palm produces clusters of flowers that can grow to be 26 ft. (8m) long.

1 MONTH	1 YEAR	2 YEARS	5 YEARS	10 YEARS	20 YEARS	30 YEARS	50 YEARS

40–75 years **Major Mitchell's cockatoo** can be found across Australia. Although most individuals die by the age of 60, at least one has lived to be 78 years old.

SUPER SCAVENGERS
Instead of hunting for live prey, condors clean up the leftovers of other predators' meals. This is called scavenging.

50–70 years **Andean condors** live in and around the Andes Mountains of South America. Their wingspan can be as great as 10.5 ft. (3.2m). This is even longer than the world's tallest man, who grew to be 8 ft. 11 in. (2.72m).

60–80 years Although many plants have both male and female parts, **American persimmon** trees (*fruit shown above*) are either male or female. The tree can only reproduce if both sexes are close together.

75 years **Horse chestnut trees** bear spiky green fruit that contain large and shiny seeds called conkers. Many of these trees are being killed by a bacterial infection called bleeding canker. Scientists are working hard to find a cure.

HOW DID HORSE CHESTNUTS GET THEIR NAME?
Horse chestnut trees were once falsely believed to be chestnuts. It was also wrongly thought that eating their nuts could help cure coughs in horses.

VERTEBRATES

| 1 MONTH | 1 YEAR | 2 YEARS | 5 YEARS | 10 YEARS | 20 YEARS | 30 YEARS | 50 YEARS |

PARROTS

Parrots live mostly in tropical regions and use their large, curved beaks to crack open seeds and nuts. They can learn human words and phrases, imitate sounds, use tools, and solve complex problems. Their bright colors and intelligence have made parrots popular as pets, but many pet parrots are taken from the wild. This has caused wild populations to decline and threatens parrot species with extinction.

*Some African gray parrots know almost 1,000 words. They are capable of meaningful conversation and **can even tell jokes**.*

*Wild parrots, like this blue-and-yellow macaw, **can fly great distances**. Their bright feathers help them blend in with tropical flowers.*

75 YEARS | 100 YEARS | 200 YEARS | 500 YEARS | 1,000 YEARS | 5,000 YEARS

THE BEST OF TIMES IS NOW

Millions of lobsters are caught each year to satisfy hungry humans, while leatherback turtles and lake sturgeons suffer when people steal their eggs. They may live to the age of 100, but some species should enjoy life while it lasts. With humans around, death could always be on the horizon . . .

LOOK RIGHT THROUGH ME!

A lobster's blood is completely transparent, or see-through. It turns blue when exposed to air.

75–100 years **Lobsters** get bigger by growing a new shell under their old one, then molting, or shedding, the older shell. Young lobsters must molt around 25 times to reach adult size.

MICROORGANISMS
PLANTS AND FUNGI
INVERTEBRATES
VERTEBRATES

50–80 years **Leatherback turtles** travel the globe in search of food and nesting grounds. One turtle was tracked by satellite over 674 days as it swam across the Pacific Ocean from Papua New Guinea to Oregon—a journey of 12,774 mi. (20,558km).

| I MONTH | I YEAR | 2 YEARS | 5 YEARS | IO YEARS | 20 YEARS | 30 YEARS | 50 YEARS |

80 years

The **silver birch** is found across much of Europe and is Finland's national tree. Its shiny silver bark contains a chemical called betulin. Scientists hope to use this in medicines to help fight obesity and to reduce the risk of heart attacks in humans.

STURGEON SAILORS

Oil from lake sturgeons was once burned as a fuel for steamboats.

80–120 years

Lake sturgeons live in the lakes and rivers of North America. They are popular food for humans, who prize their meat and also their eggs, known as caviar.

80–120 years

Southern magnolia trees bear creamy yellow flowers and a beautiful fragrance that is often used to make perfumes. In the late summer, they produce large, conelike fruit that open to reveal red seeds.

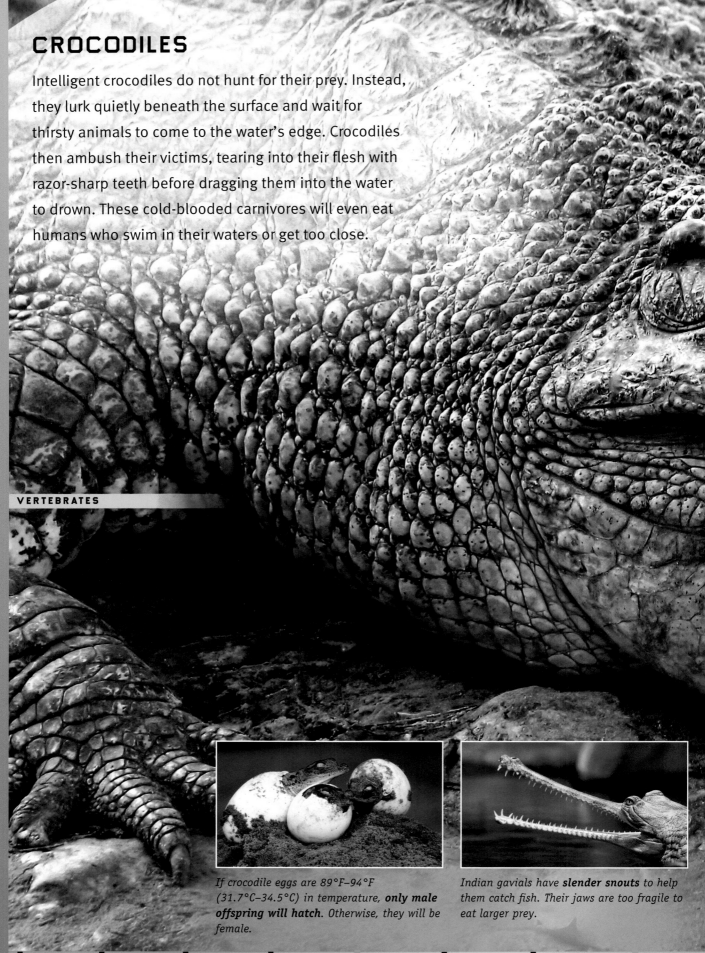

CROCODILES

Intelligent crocodiles do not hunt for their prey. Instead, they lurk quietly beneath the surface and wait for thirsty animals to come to the water's edge. Crocodiles then ambush their victims, tearing into their flesh with razor-sharp teeth before dragging them into the water to drown. These cold-blooded carnivores will even eat humans who swim in their waters or get too close.

VERTEBRATES

*If crocodile eggs are 89°F–94°F (31.7°C–34.5°C) in temperature, **only male offspring will hatch**. Otherwise, they will be female.*

*Indian gavials have **slender snouts** to help them catch fish. Their jaws are too fragile to eat larger prey.*

| 1 MONTH | 1 YEAR | 2 YEARS | 5 YEARS | 10 YEARS | 20 YEARS | 30 YEARS | 50 YEARS |

A WHALE OF A TIME

Blue whales are the largest animals on Earth, and their life span is equally enormous. When it comes to life span, however, size does not matter—you do not need to be huge to live for a hundred years. Even tiny organisms, such as the queen termite, can live for as long as a century. That's a pretty long life for something so small.

80–90 years The fruit of the **coconut palm** has many uses. Coconut flesh can be eaten, its milk can be drunk, and its oil can be used for frying.

MICROORGANISMS
PLANTS AND FUNGI
INVERTEBRATES
VERTEBRATES

80–85 years Adult **European eels** travel from all across Europe to spawn, or reproduce, in the Sargasso Sea in the middle of the Atlantic Ocean. After spawning, the adults die and the larvae drift back toward Europe.

| 1 MONTH | 1 YEAR | 2 YEARS | 5 YEARS | 10 YEARS | 20 YEARS | 30 YEARS | 50 YEARS |

50–100 years Although most termites die after one or two years, the **queen termite** can live for decades. After her death, a new queen develops in the colony.

HOW HEAVY?

A blue whale's tongue weighs 4 tons (3.6 metric tonnes)—as much as an elephant. At 130 lb. (600kg), its heart is as heavy as a small car.

80–110 years **Blue whales** are the largest animals to have ever lived on Earth. They can grow to be 100 ft. (30m) in length—as long as 2.5 school buses—and their arteries are so big that a human could swim through them.

DON'T CLEAN YOUR EARS!

Scientists can determine a blue whale's age by counting the layers of its earwax. One whale's ear contained so much wax that it was thought to be around 110 years old.

80–100 years Giant **carpet anemones** grow in a range of bright colors. These predatory creatures are highly poisonous and are able to kill many ocean species.

ON THE HUNT

When our stomachs rumble and hunger calls, we are in no doubt: we need to eat. We humans can easily go to the store, but other animals—called predators—must kill to eat. Their victims, or prey, better start running . . .

5 *Polar bears* are the largest carnivores, or meat eaters, that live on land, killing seals and even humans. They have to eat larger prey because they need more energy to live.

When an animal eats, it absorbs energy from food and it uses this to stay alive. This **Arctic food web** (*right*) shows how energy is transferred when different species eat each other.

5 *In the Arctic, the **Inuit people** eat fish, seals, and many other animals. Their remote environment and harsh climate mean the Inuit depend on hunting and fishing.*

Spiders build elaborate webs to catch their prey. Insects unwittingly fly into the web and are trapped, unable to move, until the spider comes to eat them.

5 *Killer whales*, or orcas, are the top underwater predators. They eat fish and seals. They are called apex predators because nothing naturally eats them.

4 *In the ocean, **harp seals** hunt for fish. Their sensitive whiskers help them feel for prey in murky waters.*

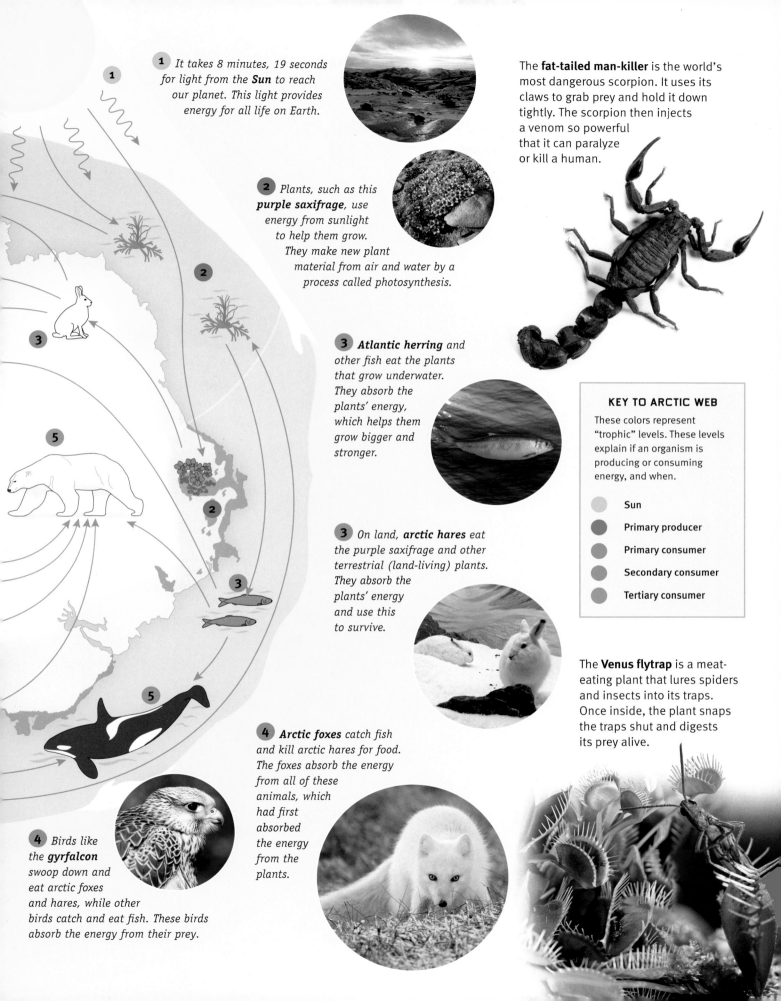

1 It takes 8 minutes, 19 seconds for light from the **Sun** to reach our planet. This light provides energy for all life on Earth.

The **fat-tailed man-killer** is the world's most dangerous scorpion. It uses its claws to grab prey and hold it down tightly. The scorpion then injects a venom so powerful that it can paralyze or kill a human.

2 Plants, such as this **purple saxifrage**, use energy from sunlight to help them grow. They make new plant material from air and water by a process called photosynthesis.

3 **Atlantic herring** and other fish eat the plants that grow underwater. They absorb the plants' energy, which helps them grow bigger and stronger.

KEY TO ARCTIC WEB

These colors represent "trophic" levels. These levels explain if an organism is producing or consuming energy, and when.

- Sun
- Primary producer
- Primary consumer
- Secondary consumer
- Tertiary consumer

3 On land, **arctic hares** eat the purple saxifrage and other terrestrial (land-living) plants. They absorb the plants' energy and use this to survive.

The **Venus flytrap** is a meat-eating plant that lures spiders and insects into its traps. Once inside, the plant snaps the traps shut and digests its prey alive.

4 **Arctic foxes** catch fish and kill arctic hares for food. The foxes absorb the energy from all of these animals, which had first absorbed the energy from the plants.

4 Birds like the **gyrfalcon** swoop down and eat arctic foxes and hares, while other birds catch and eat fish. These birds absorb the energy from their prey.

I WANT TO WALK LIKE YOU

The primates are a group of mammals that includes monkeys, apes, and prosimians. These animals are some of our closest relatives, and they hold a firm place on our family tree. Some of the primates, such as the tarsier, look very different from humans. Our closest relatives, such as the chimpanzee, look and behave a lot more like us.

The timeline shows how **primates have evolved** over the last 50 million years. Over time, different species have evolved, or changed, and broken off into new and different groups.

*Old World monkeys, such as this **patas monkey**, live in Africa and Asia. Unlike most monkeys from the New World, they can all see in full color vision.*

22 million years ago
Old World monkeys

50 million years ago
Prosimians

Tarsiers are prosimians, which means "premonkey" in Latin. They are the only entirely carnivorous, or meat-eating, primates.

35 million years ago
New World monkeys

*New World monkeys, such as this **white-faced capuchin**, are found across the Americas. They have prehensile tails that they use to grab and hold onto things.*

15 million years ago
Lesser apes

Old World monkeys, lesser apes, and great apes all have **opposable thumbs**. This means that they can move their thumbs and can use them to touch all the other fingers on their hands. This helps them hold objects.

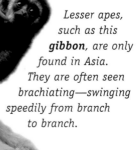

*Lesser apes, such as this **gibbon**, are only found in Asia. They are often seen brachiating—swinging speedily from branch to branch.*

When orangutans walk, they lean forward and put their weight on their fists. Gorillas (*left*) and chimpanzees **walk on their knuckles** instead, which allows them to hold things in their fingers as they move.

Humans are the only animals that always walk upright and on two legs. This type of movement is called **bipedalism.**

13 million years ago
Orangutans

Orangutans are the only Asian great apes. Dominant males develop pads on their cheeks called flanges, which tell other orangutans that they are in charge.

8 million years ago
Gorillas

Gorillas are from central Africa and are the largest of all primates. Males can weigh up to 500 lb. (230kg)—more than three adult men.

6 million years ago
Chimpanzees

Chimpanzees live in western and central Africa. They are our closest-living relatives, and our DNA is almost the same.

200,000 years ago
Humans

Modern humans are a relatively young species. Despite this, we have been able to spread out across the world and take control of our planet.

Cave paintings tell us about the ways in which our ancestors lived. Most pictures show the animals that they lived with or hunted.

DUMBING DOWN

Over the past 20,000 years, the human brain has been getting smaller. In this time, we have lost a chunk of brain about the size of an apple. Scientists are not sure why our brains have shrunk so much.

We can learn a lot about our ancestors by looking at their **skulls**. Smaller skulls tend to be much older, as the very earliest humans had smaller brains.

HUMANS

Humans are the most intelligent of all animals on Earth—even our Latin name, *Homo sapiens*, means "wise man." We can build fires, cook our own food, and make clothes and tools. Some humans have used these skills to build vast cities to live in, with impressive technology and buildings. Other humans live more traditional lifestyles in quieter corners of the globe.

VERTEBRATES

*The Bedouin people of the Middle East **travel constantly around the desert** in search of food and water.*

*The Korowai tribe of New Guinea **live in houses in the tops of trees** to escape from floods and predators.*

| I MONTH | I YEAR | 2 YEARS | 5 YEARS | IO YEARS | 20 YEARS | 30 YEARS | 50 YEARS |

HOW LONG DO WE LIVE?

Human life spans are different depending on where we live. In some parts of the world, humans are killed by natural disasters, by famine, or in wars. Although other parts of the world might be safer, some people are still at risk of an early death by eating unhealthy diets and leading inactive lives.

1 *The **Inuit of Arctic Canada** live in a very cold climate. Although their diet is quite healthy, it is also very limited: they mainly eat seals and fish. This means that their average life expectancy is shorter than that of their fellow Canadians.*

People in developed countries often eat more fatty and salty foods and consume more alcohol and sugary drinks. A **bad lifestyle** like this can lead to life-threatening problems.

2 ***Mormons** are members of a strict religious community, in which alcohol and tobacco are not allowed. Their life spans tend to be eight years longer than those of other Americans.*

CANADA

NORTH AMERICA

UNITED STATES

In developing countries, many people have little access to medical treatment and their lives are cut short by **poor health and disease**. In wealthier countries, advances in medical science can keep us alive for longer.

SOUTH AMERICA

3

BRAZIL

KEY TO MAP

This map shows the average life expectancies of the people in each country around the world.

AVERAGE LIFE EXPECTANCY BY COUNTRY IN YEARS

over 80	50–54
75–79	45–49
65–74	40–44
60–64	under 40
55–59	

BATTLE OF THE SEXES

In most countries, women tend to live longer lives than men. In the U.S., a girl born in 2012 is expected to live to be 81. A boy born on the very same day will live to be 76 years old, on average.

3 *The **tribes of the Brazilian rainforests** lead very simple and traditional lives. They hunt animals for food and use medicinal plants to treat their illnesses. Despite this, their average life spans are much shorter than in the rest of South America. They are vulnerable to outside diseases and the destruction of their homelands.*

People with **money** are able to buy better food and shelter and can purchase medications to fight off diseases. Most of the wealthiest countries are found in North America, Europe, and east Asia.

5 *Global warming and **climate change** are causing floods, droughts, crop failures, and more extreme weather. We are all at risk, but peasant farmers are the most vulnerable.*

WATCH OUT FOR MOSQUITOES!

Malaria is a life-threatening disease that is spread by mosquitoes. Two in every five people on Earth live in a malaria zone, where the disease is thought to kill a child every 30 seconds.

RUSSIA

A S I A

5

CHINA

JAPAN

6

EUROPE

ERITREA

A F R I C A

SWAZILAND

4

AUSTRALIA

6 *The Japanese have the longest average life spans in the world. This is probably due to their diet of **fish**, rice, and raw vegetables.*

A **balanced diet** containing fruit and vegetables is the key to living a longer life. Despite this, most people in poorer countries cannot afford good-quality foods. In richer countries, many people choose not to eat healthily.

Although **natural disasters** such as earthquakes often hit the headlines, their impact on the human population is low. Of the seven billion people on Earth, around 250,000 die in these tragic disasters each year. More than 1.5 million people are killed every year in car crashes.

4 *Widespread famine and diseases, such as AIDS, have significantly shortened the life spans of **people in Africa**. Swaziland, in southern Africa, has the lowest life expectancy of any country in the world. On average, people there rarely live past the age of 32.*

A STARVATION DIET

Famine is a huge problem in Africa. In the U.S., the average child eats around 3,770 calories per day—this is far too many. A child in Eritrea is lucky to eat as few as 1,600 per day.

PEOPLING THE PLANET

Today, Earth is home to more than seven billion people, with three new babies born every single second. Although our population has been growing for hundreds of years, humans have not always been reproducing so rapidly. Over time, human population growth has been affected by many events.

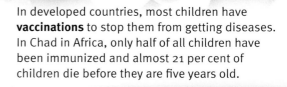

In developed countries, most children have **vaccinations** to stop them from getting diseases. In Chad in Africa, only half of all children have been immunized and almost 21 per cent of children die before they are five years old.

Not only are people on average living much longer today, but there is some evidence that they are **getting taller** as well. Scientists think that this might be as a result of better diets and health.

SPREAD THE WORD!

If every person on the planet had a copy of this book and laid them end to end, they would wrap around Earth about 48 times.

Computers, the Internet, and television have helped educate people. In developed countries, **information** about health care, food, and potential disasters is at the tips of our fingers.

2,000 years ago *Total world population is less than the total population of the U.S. today.*

10,000–7,000 years ago *Neolithic revolution: many humans switch from hunting and gathering food to growing crops and settling in villages.*

5,000 years ago *First cities are built.*

1300s *Up to 60% of all people in Europe and Asia are killed by bubonic plague (the Black Death), which was spread by fleas on rats.*

30,000–12,000 years ago *Modern human population begins to expand.*

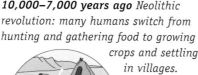

30,000–12,000 years ago

10,000–7,000 years ago

5,000 years ago

2,000 years ago

1300

YEARS

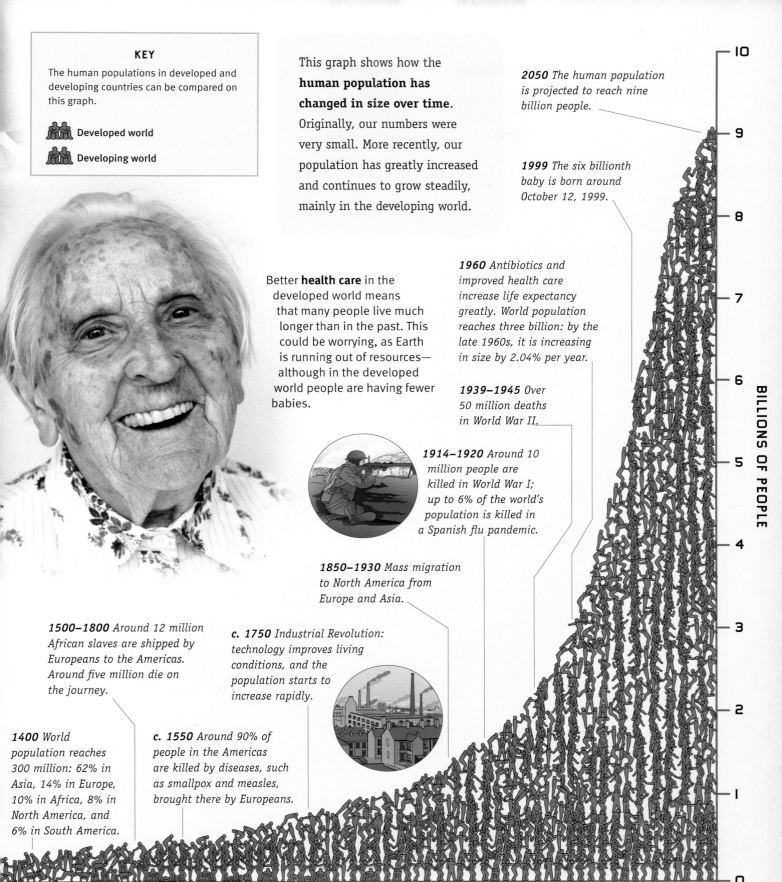

KEY

The human populations in developed and developing countries can be compared on this graph.

Developed world

Developing world

This graph shows how the **human population has changed in size over time**. Originally, our numbers were very small. More recently, our population has greatly increased and continues to grow steadily, mainly in the developing world.

2050 The human population is projected to reach nine billion people.

1999 The six billionth baby is born around October 12, 1999.

1960 Antibiotics and improved health care increase life expectancy greatly. World population reaches three billion: by the late 1960s, it is increasing in size by 2.04% per year.

1939–1945 Over 50 million deaths in World War II.

Better **health care** in the developed world means that many people live much longer than in the past. This could be worrying, as Earth is running out of resources— although in the developed world people are having fewer babies.

1914–1920 Around 10 million people are killed in World War I; up to 6% of the world's population is killed in a Spanish flu pandemic.

1850–1930 Mass migration to North America from Europe and Asia.

1500–1800 Around 12 million African slaves are shipped by Europeans to the Americas. Around five million die on the journey.

c. 1750 Industrial Revolution: technology improves living conditions, and the population starts to increase rapidly.

1400 World population reaches 300 million: 62% in Asia, 14% in Europe, 10% in Africa, 8% in North America, and 6% in South America.

c. 1550 Around 90% of people in the Americas are killed by diseases, such as smallpox and measles, brought there by Europeans.

BILLIONS OF PEOPLE

10 — 9 — 8 — 7 — 6 — 5 — 4 — 3 — 2 — 1 — 0

1400 1500 1550 1750 1800 1850 1920 1945 1960 1999 2050

YEARS

BUILDING BLOCKS OF LIFE

All living things are made of DNA, or deoxyribonucleic acid. Single units of DNA are like letters in a language. When we put lots of letters together, they make up words. When we put units of DNA together, they form genes. These genes control the way that we look and the ways in which we might develop. Our height, skin color, and some of the diseases we may catch are all determined by our genes.

A **labradoodle** is a hybrid, or mixed, breed of dog, which is born to parents of two different breeds: a Labrador retriever and a standard poodle. Labradoodles look like Labradors but are fluffy like poodles.

Long strands of DNA are tightly wound to make up **cross-shaped structures called chromosomes**. Every cell in our bodies contains a copy of these chromosomes and all of the genes wrapped around them.

KEY TO DNA

DNA is made up of two separate strands. These are joined together by pairs of chemicals, called bases. Adenine always connects with thymine, and guanine always pairs with cytosine.

- Adenine
- Thymine
- Guanine
- Cytosine

Identical twins are born when a single egg divides into two embryos. Both children have almost completely identical genes and often look very similar.

When **breeding livestock**, many farmers select animals with "good genes" to be parents. Their high-quality traits, such as big muscles and good health, might then be passed on to their offspring.

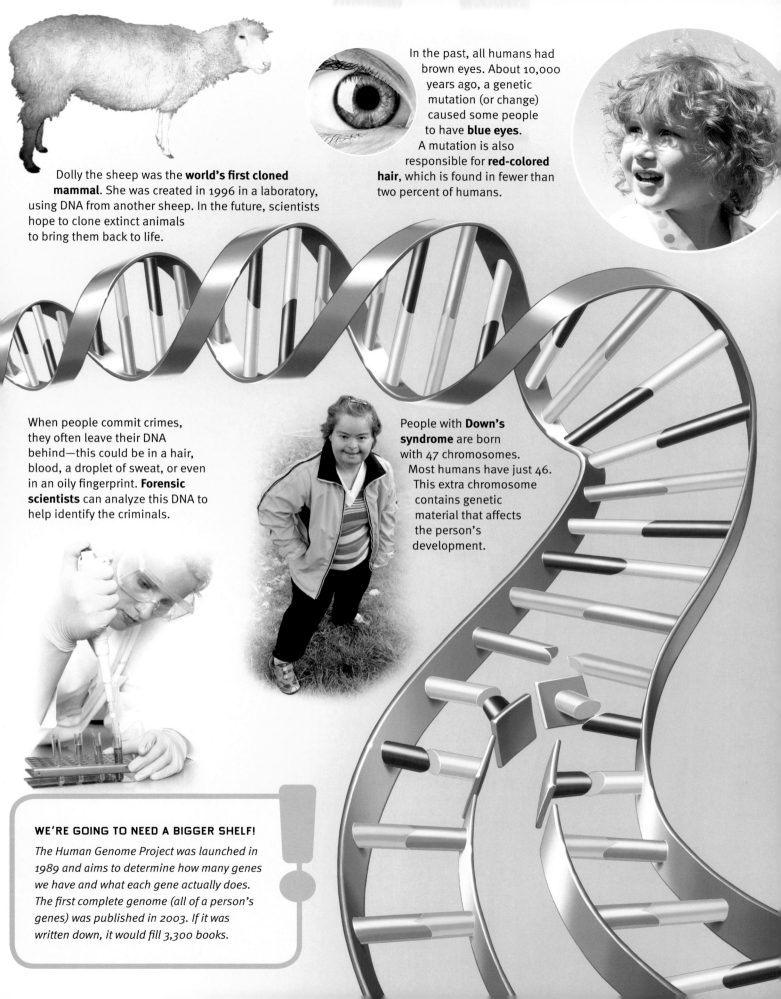

Dolly the sheep was the **world's first cloned mammal**. She was created in 1996 in a laboratory, using DNA from another sheep. In the future, scientists hope to clone extinct animals to bring them back to life.

In the past, all humans had brown eyes. About 10,000 years ago, a genetic mutation (or change) caused some people to have **blue eyes**. A mutation is also responsible for **red-colored hair**, which is found in fewer than two percent of humans.

When people commit crimes, they often leave their DNA behind—this could be in a hair, blood, a droplet of sweat, or even in an oily fingerprint. **Forensic scientists** can analyze this DNA to help identify the criminals.

People with **Down's syndrome** are born with 47 chromosomes. Most humans have just 46. This extra chromosome contains genetic material that affects the person's development.

WE'RE GOING TO NEED A BIGGER SHELF!

The Human Genome Project was launched in 1989 and aims to determine how many genes we have and what each gene actually does. The first complete genome (all of a person's genes) was published in 2003. If it was written down, it would fill 3,300 books.

IN SICKNESS AND IN HEALTH

There are millions of diseases on Earth that can make us sick. In the developed world, most people have access to health care and can go to the hospital if they become unwell. In poorer countries, the nearest doctor could be miles away, and they might not even have any medicine. In these countries, diseases are very difficult to treat and kill many more people than they do elsewhere.

KEY TO MAP

This map shows the number of new cases of tuberculosis that are reported around the world each year.

- Fewer than 50 new cases per year per 100,000 people
- 50–300 new cases
- Over 300 new cases
- No information

Tuberculosis (TB) is a deadly bacterial disease of the lungs. More than one-third of the world's population, mainly in poorer countries, is infected with tuberculosis, which causes people to cough up blood. Unless treated, the disease will kill most patients.

Obesity is when a person carries too much body fat for their height and sex. Too much fat can badly affect health by increasing the risk of heart disease and diabetes. It can also cause mental illness if patients are unhappy with their weight.

Diabetes occurs when a person's body stops making insulin or does not make enough. Insulin is needed to help convert glucose, or blood sugar, into fuel for the body's cells. People with diabetes have too much glucose in their blood and often need to inject themselves with insulin. They have to test their blood sugar levels each day (*below*).

FIGHT THE FAT!

Obesity can be treated with a healthy, balanced diet and plenty of exercise to help the patient burn fat and lose weight.

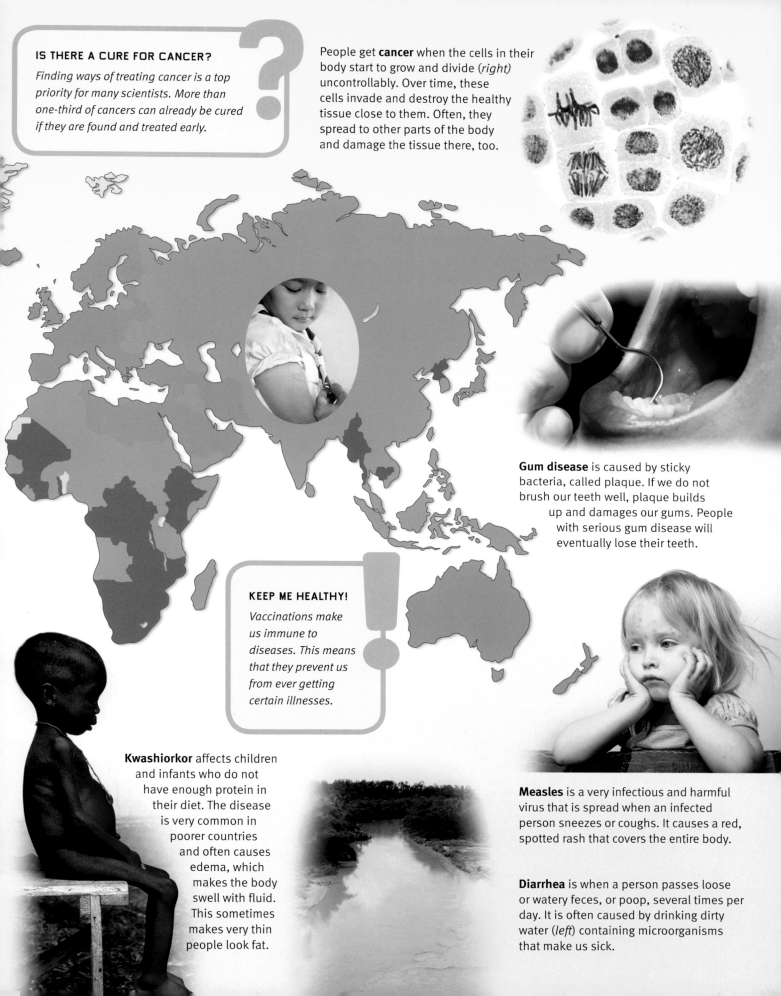

IS THERE A CURE FOR CANCER?

Finding ways of treating cancer is a top priority for many scientists. More than one-third of cancers can already be cured if they are found and treated early.

People get **cancer** when the cells in their body start to grow and divide (*right*) uncontrollably. Over time, these cells invade and destroy the healthy tissue close to them. Often, they spread to other parts of the body and damage the tissue there, too.

Gum disease is caused by sticky bacteria, called plaque. If we do not brush our teeth well, plaque builds up and damages our gums. People with serious gum disease will eventually lose their teeth.

KEEP ME HEALTHY!

Vaccinations make us immune to diseases. This means that they prevent us from ever getting certain illnesses.

Kwashiorkor affects children and infants who do not have enough protein in their diet. The disease is very common in poorer countries and often causes edema, which makes the body swell with fluid. This sometimes makes very thin people look fat.

Measles is a very infectious and harmful virus that is spread when an infected person sneezes or coughs. It causes a red, spotted rash that covers the entire body.

Diarrhea is when a person passes loose or watery feces, or poop, several times per day. It is often caused by drinking dirty water (*left*) containing microorganisms that make us sick.

THIS IS PLANET EARTH

Only humans have the power to manipulate our planet and to exploit Earth's resources. While this might make our own lives easier, doing so comes at a cost. Taking control of our planet can affect the fate of all the other life forms that share our world.

TREAD LIGHTLY!

Humanity's ecological footprint is 1.5 planet Earths. This means that Earth needs to be 1.5 times larger than it actually is if all humans are to have enough resources to survive.

Humans have so many lights on at night that **big cities can be seen from space** (*right*). This satellite image also shows us where most people live.

KEY TO MAP

This map shows ten of the world's largest megacities. Each is home to more than 20 million people.

1. **Tokyo** 34.3 million
2. **Guangzhou** 25.2 million
3. **Seoul** 25.1 million
4. **Shanghai** 24.8 million
5. **Delhi** 23.3 million
6. **Mumbai** 23 million
7. **Mexico City** 22.9 million
8. **New York** 22 million
9. **São Paulo** 20.9 million
10. **Manila** 20.3 million

As much as 80 percent of the world's population relies on **medicinal plants**. This plant, called quinine (*right*), can be used to treat malaria. Like many other important plants, it is threatened by deforestation.

Scientists have **genetically modified crops,** such as corn (*left*) and barley (*right*), to help them grow quicker and be resistant to disease. Many people are concerned that this is interfering with nature.

In China, most people in big cities are **only allowed to have one child**. This law helps stop urban areas from becoming too overcrowded.

Most cities are **home to millions of people**, even if the cities are not very big. Wealthy people often live alongside poorer people. Their quality of life is very different.

More than 884 million people have **no access to drinking water**—that is one in eight people on Earth. Many must travel for miles each day to find clean water.

Almost 30 million people rely on water from Lake Chad in Africa. **Global warming** has shrunk the lake to one-fifth of its original size in less than 40 years.

In the developed world, we often have access to plenty of water. Humans have built **giant dams** to control floods, generate power, and provide water for growing crops.

The U.S. Navy has trained sea lions and **dolphins** to help out in military operations. Sea lions have excellent underwater vision and are used to locate enemy divers. Dolphins such as this one have been trained to find and mark underwater mines, or bombs.

Sea turtles spend almost their entire lives at sea, except for females, who come ashore to lay their eggs. They normally do this on the same beach every year. Often, this is the beach that they hatched on themselves. When baby sea turtles hatch, they know immediately to head for the ocean.

The world's **oldest ever person** was Jeanne Calment of France. She was born on February 21, 1875 and lived for 122 years and 164 days, before her death on August 4, 1997.

Elephants are among the few animals that can recognize themselves in a mirror, along with the great apes, some dolphins and whales, and a small number of birds. Most other animals are afraid of their reflections. They do not realize that the mirror shows an image of themselves and believe it is a rival or predator.

Killer whales, or orcas, hunt in groups and work together to kill large prey. Despite their smaller size, they have been known to attack adult blue whales, drown baby whales, called calves, and even kill great white sharks.

TIME IS ON MY SIDE

5

100–5,000+ YEARS

YOU'VE GOT MAIL

In many countries, you can look forward to a birthday card from the monarch or president if you live to be 100. In Ireland they will send you some money, and in Japan you will get a silver cup. Other species might not get any presents, but they still have reason to celebrate.

HAPPY HUNDREDTH!

Humans who live to be 100 years old are called centenarians. People who live to see their 110th birthday are called supercentenarians.

100 years

The **olm**, or human fish, is a blind salamander that lives in the caves of Slovenia and Croatia. With a life span of over a century, this odd creature is the world's longest-living amphibian. Scientists are not sure why the olm lives for so long, as such small organisms normally die much sooner.

MICROORGANISMS
PLANTS AND FUNGI
INVERTEBRATES
VERTEBRATES

100 years

One of the world's largest **giant clams** was found near Japan in 1956. When alive, it would have weighed around 750 lb. (340kg)—almost as much as five men.

100–205 years

Rougheye rockfish are found in the north Pacific Ocean and are among the world's longest-living fish. They take their name from a series of sharp spines along the lower rim of their eyes. Their lives are often cut short by commercial fishing operations that catch wild rockfish for people to eat.

100–150 years

Fig trees produce edible fruit that have been eaten by people for thousands of years. Some historians believe that these plants were the first to be cultivated by humans. Ancient figs found buried in the Jordan Valley in the Middle East are probably about 11,400 years old.

200 years

Red sea urchins are completely covered in sharp, spiky spines. They use these as stilts to move around and as protection from predators. Most of the oldest sea urchins have been found off the western Canadian coast, between Vancouver Island and the mainland.

100–200 years

The **jojoba** shrub is native to the Mojave and Sonoran deserts of California, Arizona, and Mexico. Its seeds produce a natural wax, called jojoba oil, which is used in cosmetics and in traditional medicines.

75 YEARS   **100** YEARS   **200** YEARS   **500** YEARS   **1,000** YEARS   **5,000** YEARS

GIANT TORTOISES

Giant tortoises live on the islands of the Seychelles, near Africa, and the Galápagos, near South America. These tortoises are highly endangered, with many populations hunted close to extinction by hungry sailors who killed them for food. Today, they are fiercely protected. Although most live to be around 100 years old, some are thought to live for 250 years or more.

VERTEBRATES

When threatened, tortoises **pull their head and legs inside their shell** so that predators cannot grab them.

At around 100 years old, Lonesome George was the last of the Pinta Island tortoises. **His subspecies is now extinct.**

THE WEIRD AND WONDERFUL

One of these species has not changed very much since dinosaurs roamed the planet. Another can squirt out waste through a tube, while yet another has the biggest mouth on Earth. To each other, these species might be perfectly normal—but to us, they are beautifully bizarre.

140–160 years
Geoduck clams have a long, gooey siphon, or tube, that can be up to 3 ft. (1m) in length. They feed by sucking water up through the siphon, filtering out food, and then squirting out the waste.

MICROORGANISMS
PLANTS AND FUNGI
INVERTEBRATES
VERTEBRATES

150–210 years
The **bowhead whale** is found in and around Arctic waters. It has the largest mouth of any animal on Earth. Its tongue alone can grow to be 16 ft. (5m) long and 10 ft. (3m) wide—so big that you could park a large car on it.

HEADS UP

A bowhead whale's head takes up more than one-third of its entire body.

| MONTH | I YEAR | 2 YEARS | 5 YEARS | IO YEARS | 20 YEARS | 30 YEARS | 50 YEARS |

60–200 years

Tuataras are reptiles that are found only in New Zealand. They are the last surviving members of a group called Sphenodontia. This group first walked on Earth about 200 million years ago.

200 years

The **coco de mer** palm produces the biggest seeds of any plant in the world. A single seed can weigh as much as 66 lb. (30kg)—about the same as a large penguin.

250 years

Both a male tree (with red catkins) and a female tree (with green catkins) are needed in order for **black poplar** trees to reproduce. Only 2,500 trees are left in Great Britain, and fewer than 400 are female. They are also found elsewhere across Europe and in central Asia.

KOI FISH

Koi fish are domesticated versions of the common carp. Over hundreds of years, they have been bred for ornamental, or decorative, purposes and now come in a vast range of bright colors and patterns. The oldest ever koi, named Hanako, was thought to be 226 years old. This would make koi fish the longest-living vertebrates.

VERTEBRATES

*Koi have **hooklike barbels** at the corners of their mouths, which they use to taste their food.*

*In Japanese culture, koi are **symbols of peace and strength**. They are often seen in ponds in traditional gardens.*

THE PARTY'S OVER

Many different species are threatened or endangered. This means that their populations are so small that they are at risk of becoming extinct. Extinction occurs when the very last member of a species dies out. Once a species is extinct, it is gone forever.

This diagram (*right*) highlights the different things that **threaten and endanger species**. Several threats are entirely natural, such as a meteorite hitting Earth from space. Most, however, are caused by humans. We are often to blame when a species becomes extinct.

*Natural disasters, such as a **meteor impact**, could wipe out life on Earth.*

Dodoes were large, flightless birds that lived on the island of Mauritius in the Indian Ocean. Humans hunted them to extinction in the 1600s.

*When land is cleared for **farming**, species that lived there have nowhere to go.*

*Many species have been **hunted** to extinction by humans.*

***Logging** destroys forests and kills the species within them.*

About 64 percent of all known plants are threatened with extinction. Although many plants are killed by diseases, most are being **cut down** by humans.

The **Florida torreya** is a very rare tree. Most specimens have been killed by fungal infections that stop them from reproducing.

PLANTS
64%

ARE SOME SPECIES MORE AT RISK THAN OTHERS?

Yes. Scientists put species into different groups, depending on how much at risk they are. The most serious is "Critically Endangered" for species close to extinction. This is followed by "Endangered," "Vulnerable," "Near Threatened," and "Least Concern."

At least 20 percent of all known vertebrate species are threatened with extinction. Most are affected by **habitat loss**, when humans destroy their homes. Many others are hunted for food.

The **Javan rhinoceros** once lived across much of Asia. Today, fewer than 60 are left. The others were hunted for their horns.

Only 280 **Cross River gorillas** are left in Cameroon and Nigeria in Africa. All the others were killed by hunting and by habitat loss.

*Global warming is **melting icecaps and glaciers**. This is raising sea levels and flooding fragile habitats.*

__Pollution__ from factories affects air quality, making it difficult to breathe. It also contaminates rivers, lakes, and seas.

__Burning fossil fuels__ is damaging the environment.

__Harmful waste__ from big cities often ends up in rivers, lakes, and seas.

__Overfishing__ threatens many species of fish. Other marine animals are often caught in nets.

The last **Tasmanian wolf**, or thylacine, died in a zoo on September 7, 1936. Wild Tasmanian wolves were hunted to extinction by humans for killing domestic sheep.

Around 29 percent of all known invertebrate species are at serious risk of extinction. Many are affected by **pollution and pesticides**. Others are killed by non-native predators that humans have introduced.

Atlantic bluefin tuna are highly prized for food: in 2001, a single tuna sold for $217,000 at Tokyo's Tsukiji fish market. As a result of overfishing to meet demand, these tuna now face extinction.

Pacific walrus are threatened by climate change. Because Arctic ice is melting into warmer seas, these walrus have nowhere to rest and reproduce.

INVERTEBRATES

29%

DEFYING GRAVITY

Some species, such as the mountain ash, grow to dizzying heights and seem to have no limits. Others, like the bonsai, only grow into little trees. They may be hugely different in size, but this does not affect their life spans. All of these plants live for similar lengths of time, and some might even grow to be 1,000 years old.

300–400 years Eucalyptus oil is produced by the leaves of the **Tasmanian blue gum** tree. The oil is used to treat coughs and colds, but large amounts are very toxic and the oil can be harmful if eaten. Koalas have developed immunity to this and can eat the tree's leaves without becoming sick.

100–500 years **Bonsai** trees are normal trees that have been specially cut and shaped to keep them small. In ancient Japan, allowing a tree to grow naturally was not considered a very caring thing to do. Instead, it was believed that creating a bonsai showed love and affection for the tree.

MICROORGANISMS
PLANTS AND FUNGI
INVERTEBRATES
VERTEBRATES

300–400 years A red **sugar maple** leaf is the national symbol of Canada and takes pride of place on the Canadian flag. Maple syrup is made by tapping, or collecting, sap from the trunk of the maple tree (*far left*). The sap is then boiled into a thick syrup.

| MONTH | I YEAR | 2 YEARS | 5 YEARS | IO YEARS | 20 YEARS | 30 YEARS | 50 YEARS |

400–450 years

The **mountain ash** is the tallest flowering plant on Earth. The world's biggest lives in Tasmania and is 330 ft. (100m) tall—that's twice the length of an Olympic swimming pool.

KNEE DEEP

Bald cypress trees grow knee-shaped roots that come out of the water. This helps the roots get some air.

600 years

Bald cypress trees (*right*) often grow in or close to lakes and rivers. They distribute their seeds by dropping them onto the water. The seeds float to the shore and germinate, or sprout into seedlings.

FLYING NUTS

Each year, the U.S. produces enough pecan nuts to fill 480 passenger planes.

300 years

The name of the **pecan** tree was originally used by the First Nations native people of Canada. They cultivated pecans before the 1500s. In the Algonquin language, the word "pecan" means "a nut that must be cracked with a stone."

75 YEARS   **100** YEARS   **200** YEARS   **500** YEARS   **1,000** YEARS   **5,000** YEARS

OCEAN QUAHOGS

Ocean quahogs are hard clams that live in the Atlantic Ocean. Many quahogs live to be 250 years old, but some can live for centuries longer. The oldest ever recorded was found off the coast of Iceland and is thought to be more than 500 years old. Scientists can determine the age of a quahog by counting the growth bands within its shell.

INVERTEBRATES

To eat small quahogs, **starfish wrap their arms around them**, push their stomach out through their mouth, and digest them.

Quahogs **bury themselves in the sediment on the seabed** to hide from predators. Only their mouth and anus are visible.

| 1 MONTH | 1 YEAR | 2 YEARS | 5 YEARS | 10 YEARS | 20 YEARS | 30 YEARS | 50 YEARS |

GIANTS IN THE SKY

The giant sequoia grows bigger than any other tree on Earth, while the coast redwood is the tallest living thing on the planet. Like all of these species, their life spans are enormous to match.

2,000–3,000 years The world's largest **giant sequoia** tree, named General Sherman, is found in California. It would take around 20 people holding hands to completely surround its trunk.

1,000–2,000 years **Welwitschia** plants are only found in Namibia and Angola, in southwestern Africa. Despite living in a hot and dry desert climate, they can survive for thousands of years.

MICROORGANISMS
PLANTS AND FUNGI
INVERTEBRATES
VERTEBRATES

2,300 years **Giant barrel sponges** are often called the "redwoods of the reef." This is because their life span underwater is similar to that of redwood trees on land.

| 1 MONTH | 1 YEAR | 2 YEARS | 5 YEARS | 10 YEARS | 20 YEARS | 30 YEARS | 50 YEARS |

1,000–3,000 years

A **coast redwood** called Hyperion is the tallest tree in the world. It has grown to be more than 377 ft. (115m)—about as tall as 25 giraffes. Scientists think that the tree could have grown even taller if the top had not been damaged by woodpeckers. Hyperion's exact location is a secret, but it is probably in northern California.

2,400 years

The parasitic fungus *Armillaria solidipes* is very damaging to trees. Infected trees must be cut down to stop the fungus from spreading.

2,000–4,000 years

Ginkgo biloba trees have not changed their appearance very much in over 270 million years. For this reason, they are called "living fossils." In some countries, the white seeds of these trees are cooked and eaten, and their leaves are often used to help treat diseases.

3,000 years

Yaretas are tiny, bright-green flowering plants that grow on the mountains of South America. Because they catch fire easily, they are used by local people as fuel.

2,000–5,000 years

Some **yew** trees may be as old as 5,000 years, but there is no way for scientists to check this. Unlike most trees, their trunks hollow out over time, so we cannot count their growth rings to see how old they are. Most parts of a yew tree are poisonous, except for the bright-red covers that surround their seeds. These help attract birds that eat the seeds and spread them out in their feces, or poop.

BRISTLECONE PINES

Bristlecone pines are the oldest nonclonal organisms on Earth. This means that they do not clone themselves in order to extend their life span. At present, the world's oldest tree is nicknamed Methuselah and is more than 4,840 years old. To protect it, the tree's exact location is kept a secret.

PLANTS AND FUNGI

| MONTH | I YEAR | 2 YEARS | 5 YEARS | IO YEARS | 20 YEARS | 30 YEARS | 50 YEARS |

Until it was cut down in 1964 for scientific research, Prometheus was the **world's oldest tree,** at 4,862 years old.

Bristlecone pines are found in the western U.S. This young sapling could grow to be **more than 5,000 years old.**

75 YEARS   **100** YEARS   **200** YEARS   **500** YEARS   **1,000** YEARS   **5,000** YEARS

I WILL SURVIVE

Some of these species have cloned themselves, making genetically identical copies of their cells in order to live for longer. Others have been frozen alive for millions of years, waiting to thaw out. These record-breaking species have lived for longer than anything else on Earth. After 5,000 years or more, most are still with us—and here to stay.

9,550 years The **Norway spruce** originally came from Europe but is now widely grown across North America. One tree, called Old Tjikko, lives in Sweden and is one of the oldest trees in the world. It has cloned its roots repeatedly in order to extend its life span.

MICROORGANISMS
PLANTS AND FUNGI
INVERTEBRATES
VERTEBRATES

5,000– 13,000 years The **box huckleberry** shrub is found across North America. One colony in Pennsylvania is thought to have been cloning itself for as long as 13,000 years. This makes it old enough to have survived the last ice age.

WE NEED A BIGGER POT!

A single box huckleberry colony consists of only one plant, but it can grow to be many miles long.

| MONTH | I YEAR | 2 YEARS | 5 YEARS | IO YEARS | 20 YEARS | 30 YEARS | 50 YEARS |

500,000 years Scientists drilled this core of permafrost, or permanently frozen soil, in northeastern Siberia. One of the cores contained microscopic **actinobacteria**, which were still alive after being trapped in the ice for half a million years.

11,700 years This **creosote bush** (*below*) lives in the Mojave Desert in the Southwest. It has earned the nickname "King Clone," as the plant has been cloning itself for almost 12,000 years.

80,000 years One **quaking aspen** tree, called Pando, has been cloning itself for so long that it now weighs 6,610 tons (6,000 metric tonnes)— more than 1,100 elephants. It is found in the state of Utah.

43,600 years **King's lomatia** is a shrub that is only found in Tasmania. Only 500 of these plants are left in the wild, and they are all genetically identical clones.

250 million years These ancient bacteria (*right*) are the oldest living things on Earth. After 250 million years, they were found buried alive in salt crystals taken from a mine in New Mexico. Scientists plan to call them ***Virgibacillus permians***.

75 YEARS   **100** YEARS   **200** YEARS   **500** YEARS   **1,000** YEARS   **5,000** YEARS

CORAL REEFS

Corals are tiny animals that live in colonies in the oceans. They release a chemical called calcium carbonate, which builds up over thousands of years to form giant structures called reefs. Most of Australia's Great Barrier Reef is 10,000 years old, but some sections date back more than 18 million years. This reef is the largest on Earth.

INVERTEBRATES

The **Great Barrier Reef** is the only living thing that is big enough to be seen from space.

The **crown-of-thorns starfish** destroys corals by climbing onto reefs and digesting them.

WHO WANTS TO LIVE FOREVER?

Some people are going to extraordinary lengths to help humans live a little longer. Scientists are working hard to find cures for deadly diseases, while some governments are looking to outer space in order to save humankind. Others are more concerned about saving themselves and just hope to live for longer than anybody else.

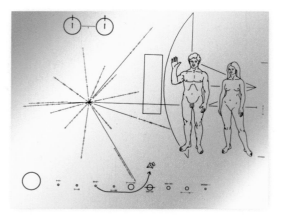

Two identical **Pioneer plaques** were launched into space in the early 1970s. Their symbols are a code that explains the existence of humankind and were sent as a message for extraterrestrial (alien) life. Nobody has replied . . . yet.

Some scientists are trying to **"grow" new organs and limbs**. In one famous experiment, human cells were injected into an ear-shaped mold. These cells were then grown on the back of a laboratory mouse.

Some humans have chosen to be frozen after death in a process called **cryopreservation**. They plan to be thawed out at some point in the future, once science has advanced and can bring them back to life.

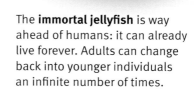

The **immortal jellyfish** is way ahead of humans: it can already live forever. Adults can change back into younger individuals an infinite number of times.

Scientists can now **grow meat** that has never been part of a living animal. Although the process is very expensive, this might mean that in the future animals will no longer have to be reared and slaughtered to provide us with food.

Science-fiction movies such as *Star Trek* have described **artificial space colonies** and the possibility of humans moving to other planets. As the human population grows and uses up the Earth's resources, these ideas might become a reality—but only in the distant future.

One 2,400-year-old colony of **Armillaria solidipes** fungi is thought to be the largest in the world. It covers more than 3.4 sq. mi. (8.8km²) of the Malheur National Forest in Oregon, although most of the colony is hidden underground. In the fall, it produces thousands of mushrooms that are visible on the surface.

The **albatross** has an excellent sense of smell. When scientists poured bacon fat into the ocean, they found that some species could smell it as far as 18 mi. (29km) away.

More than one million **Mexican free-tailed bats** live under the Congress Avenue Bridge in Austin, Texas—they form the largest urban bat colony in North America. Every night, they fly off in search of insects to eat and then return to the bridge before sunrise each day.

Roses are known for their beautiful flowers that grow at the end of spiky, thorn-covered stems. Because roses are perennial plants, they have no definite life span and will continue living, given the right conditions. One rose, in the garden of St. Mary's Cathedral in Hildesheim, Germany, is thought to have been growing for more than 1,000 years. This would make it the oldest in the world.

The **giant potato cod** is found mostly off the coasts of Australia and Asia. It can grow up to 7 ft. (2m) in length and weigh as much as 243 lb. (110kg)—far bigger than the average human. These fish are very territorial and fiercely aggressive.

GLOSSARY

These pages provide brief explanations of technical terms used in the book.

Ammonite An extinct aquatic animal that is often found as a fossil.

Amoeba A single-celled microorganism that constantly changes its shape.

Amphibian A cold-blooded vertebrate animal that lives on land and in water, such as a frog.

Angiosperm A flowering plant.

Annual plant A plant that lives for only one year.

Arboreal Describes an organism that lives in trees.

Arthropod An invertebrate animal that has a hard external skeleton, jointed limbs, and a segmented body. Arthropods include crabs and scorpions.

Bacteria Simple, single-celled microorganisms.

Biennial plant A plant that lives for only two years.

Biodiversity The variety of different species in a habitat.

Bipedalism The ability to walk upright and on two legs.

Carnivore An organism that eats meat.

Carotenoids A group of red- and yellow-colored pigments that are found in some plants and crustaceans. Flamingos absorb these pigments from the food that they eat, which turns their feathers pink.

Cephalopod A group of marine animals including the squid, nautilus, octopus, and cuttlefish.

Chlorophyll A group of green-colored pigments found in plants, which absorb light energy from the Sun.

Cloning The process of creating an organism that is genetically identical to another organism.

Coniferous tree A tree or shrub that has needles and cones.

Crustacean A group of arthropods that includes crabs, lobsters, and millipedes, among others.

Cryopreservation The process of freezing a dead body to protect it over a long period of time.

Deciduous tree A tree or plant that loses its leaves in the fall each year.

Deforestation The process of cutting down trees to completely destroy a forest.

DNA Deoxyribonucleic acid. This is a molecule that forms the genetic code of most living organisms.

Extinction The permanent dying-out of a species.

Flange A large pad on the cheek of an orangutan.

Fossil The preserved remains of an ancient or prehistoric organism.

Fungi A group of species that includes mushrooms, molds, and yeasts.

Gene A length of DNA that contains the code for a specific trait or purpose.

Genetic mutation A change in an organism's genetic code.

Genetically modified An organism that has had its DNA deliberately altered.

Genome An organism's entire genetic code.

Habitat The place where an organism lives.

Hermaphrodite An organism that has both male and female sexual organs.

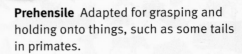

Hominin The group that includes modern humans and extinct humans.

Host An organism infected with a parasite.

Hybrid An offspring of two parents who are of different species or subspecies.

Imago A winged, adult form—the final developmental stage in the life cycle of many invertebrates.

Invertebrate An animal that has no backbone, or spinal column.

Larva The second developmental stage in the life cycle of many invertebrates.

Life cycle The series of developmental changes that an organism goes through during its life.

Life span The number of years that an organism might live.

Mammal A warm-blooded vertebrate with hair or fur and that breathes air. Mothers produce milk to feed their young.

Marsupial A female mammal with a pouch on her stomach, in which her offspring live and drink milk until fully developed. Marsupials include kangaroos.

Microorganism A species that is often too small to be seen with the naked eye.

Monotreme A mammal that lays eggs, such as the platypus.

Parasite An organism that lives in or on another organism in order to survive.

Perennial plant A plant with no fixed life span that will continue living if conditions are right.

Permafrost Permanently frozen soil.

Pollinator An animal that carries pollen from the male part of a flower to the female part.

Predator An organism that hunts and kills for food.

Prehensile Adapted for grasping and holding onto things, such as some tails in primates.

Primate A group of mammals that includes humans, apes, monkeys, and prosimians.

Proboscis A trunk or nose.

Prosimian A very primitive type of primate, such as lemurs and tarsiers.

Pseudopod The part of an amoeba's body that extends forward to help it move.

Pupa The third developmental stage in the life cycle of many invertebrates.

Radiometric dating A method for determining how old rocks and fossils are.

Reptile A cold-blooded vertebrate whose skin is covered in scales, such as a snake or lizard.

Rhizobia A group of microorganisms that live in the soil and swap nutrients with plants.

Rotifer A group of microorganisms that live in fresh and saltwater habitats.

Savanna An open, grassy area that is scattered with trees and shrubs.

Sexual dimorphism When a species has two distinct and separate male and female forms.

Tetrapod A vertebrate animal that has four limbs.

Tundra A cold and treeless habitat found near the poles.

Vertebrate An animal that has a backbone, or spinal column.

INDEX

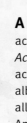

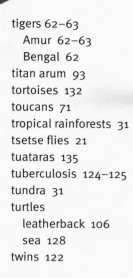

ACKNOWLEDGMENTS

Academic consultants

The author would like to thank the following for their invaluable assistance:

Kate Auckland Primate Immunogenetics and Molecular Ecology (PrIME) Research Group, Division of Biological Anthropology, University of Cambridge, U.K. | **Dr. Paco Bertolani** Leverhulme Centre for Human Evolutionary Studies (LCHES), Division of Biological Anthropology, University of Cambridge, U.K. | **Dr. Paul Butler** School of Ocean Sciences, Bangor University, U.K. | **Dr. Susana Carvalho** Leverhulme Centre for Human Evolutionary Studies (LCHES), Division of Biological Anthropology, University of Cambridge, U.K. | **Dr. Tom Flower** Behavioural Ecology Group, Department of Zoology, University of Cambridge, U.K. | **Dr. Rie Goto** Human Epidemiology Nutrition Growth Ecology (HENGE) Research Group, Division of Biological Anthropology, University of Cambridge, U.K. | **H. Ross Hawkins, Ph.D.** Founder and Executive Director, the Hummingbird Society | **Dr. Lucy E. King** Save the Elephants, Nairobi, Kenya | **Dr. L. A. Knapp** Primate Immunogenetics and Molecular Ecology (PrIME) Research Group, Division of Biological Anthropology, University of Cambridge, U.K. | **Suha Mahayni** Primate Immunogenetics and Molecular Ecology (PrIME) Research Group, Division of Biological Anthropology, University of Cambridge, U.K. | **Dr. Martha Nelson-Flower** DST/NRF Centre of Excellence at the Percy FitzPatrick Institute, University of Cape Town, South Africa | **Prof. Dr. Stefano Piraino, Ph.D.** Dipartimento Scienze e Tecnologie, Biologiche ed Ambientali (DiSTeBa), University of Salento, Italy | **Dr. Barry Rice** Sierra College and Center for Plant Diversity, University of California at Davis, U.S. | **Frances Rivera** Leverhulme Centre for Human Evolutionary Studies (LCHES), Division of Biological Anthropology, University of Cambridge, U.K. | **Dr. Fred Rumsey** Botany Department, Angela Marmont Centre, Natural History Museum, London, U.K. | **Prof. Dr. Anne E. Russon** Psychology Department, Glendon College, York University, Toronto, Canada | **Dr. Martin Sayer** NERC National Facility for Scientific Diving & Dunstaffnage Hyperbaric Unit, Scottish Association for Marine Science, Dunbeg, Oban, Argyll, U.K. | **Ronda Schwetz** Interim Director, Henry Vilas Zoo, Madison, Wisconsin, U.S. | **Professor James Scourse** School of Ocean Sciences, Bangor University, U.K. | **Dr. Gerald J Seiler** U.S. Department of Agriculture, Agricultural Research Service, Fargo, North Dakota, U.S. | **B. J. Turton** Primate Immunogenetics and Molecular Ecology (PrIME) Research Group, Division of Biological Anthropology, University of Cambridge, U.K. | **Dr. Joseph P. Vacanti, M.D.** Tissue Engineering & Organ Fabrication Lab, Massachusetts General Hospital, Boston, Massachusetts, U.S. | **Prof. Dr. Russell H. Vreeland** U.S. Biological Applied Research Consortium, Belle Haven, Virginia, U.S. | **Dr. Joshua M. Ward** Department of Psychiatry, Harvard Medical School, Boston, Massachusetts, U.S. | **Prof. Dr. Eske Willerslev** Centre for GeoGenetics, University of Copenhagen, Denmark | **Vanessa A. D. Wilson** School of Philosophy, Psychology and Language Sciences, University of Edinburgh, U.K.

The author would also like to acknowledge his appreciation to the following for their extensive advice and contributions:

Diane Ager | Kirtana Ahluwalia | Samantha Alexander | Nathan Arboleda | Marie Banes | Leslie Banes | Wendy Banes | Eddie Banes | Amalia Bastos | Bill Brown | Julie Brown | Roy Burkin | Maureen Burkin | Katherine Christopher | Mark Ciccone | Eric Ciccone | Suzi Clements | Regina Cooper | Ann Cundick | Keith Cundick | AnDr.ea Defilló Conde | Anders Fisher | Olive Fort | Mike Gołowczyński | Vick Guthrie | SU.S.n Hollander | Bill Jacobs | Linda Jacobs | Ryan Jacobs | Donna Kassewitz | Jack Kassewitz | Tamar Law | Nicole Leal | Alexander Lu | Yan Lin Lye | Victoria Montecillo | Gaile Parkin | Jessica Pisarek | Ellen Powell | Zara Rabinovitch | Ryan Reiss | Ronda Schwetz | Joe Seibert | Anne Shaw | Barb Shaw | Carol Marguerite Slater | Derek Slater | Lynne M Steinkamp | Tom Suddards | Maggie Suddards | Veronica K. Thomas | Zoë Torres | Deidra Wirakusumah | Alistair Wong

Heritage Editorial would like to thank Tina Vaughan, Tim Streater, and George Heritage for their contribution to the initial development of this book.

Picture acknowledgments

The publishers would like to thank the following for permission to reproduce their material. Every care has been taken to trace copyright holders. If there have been unintentional omissions or failure to trace copyright holders, then we apologize and will endeavor to make corrections in any future editions.

All photos are courtesy of Shutterstock unless otherwise stated.

Key: b = bottom, c = center, l = left, r = right, t = top

FLPA—Frank Lane Picture Agency
Naturepl—Nature Picture Library

Cover tl to r (all Shutterstock): Peter Waters; Peter Gyure; Mircea Bezergheanu; Johann Swanepoel; Peter Waters; Aleksandr Kurganov; Gertjan Hooljer; Hallgerd; Dobermaraner. Cover cl to r (all Shutterstock): Dusan Zidar; chantal de bruijne; Sebastian Duda. Cover bl to r (all Shutterstock): Vlad61; Eric Isselee; michaeljung; Kokhanchikov; camellia; ivosar; Martin Valigursky; Eric Isselee; Eric Isselee; geraldb; Ilya Akinshin; Eric Isselee; Chesapeake Images; alslutsky. Back cover: tr andersphoto; c Lynn Whitt; bc Marcus VDT; bcr Eric Isselee; br Sergii Figurnyi. Spine: t Eric Isselee; c Jason Stitt; b Irin-k. Front flap t Eric Isselee; b Hector Conesa. Back flap t maragu; b palko72. 12tr Kenneth Todar, University of Wisconsin-Madison, U.S.; 12bl Wikipedia/Rocky Mountain Laboratories, NIAID, NIH, U.S.; 12cr Wikipedia/Jasper Nance; 13bl Wikipedia/J J. Harrison; 14cl Wim van Egmond; 14–15 Wim van Egmond; 17tc FLPA; 17tr FLPA; 17cl FLPA; 20tr FLPA; 21tl Naturepl; 25bl Rutgers University, U.S./Uwe Kils; 21br NOAA, U.S.; 27tr Wikipedia/Glen Fergus; 27bc FLPA; 27bl Wikipedia/Piotr Naskecki; 32tl Robert Svensson/msitua.net; 32cr Wikipedia/C. Lalueza Fox, I Agnarsson, M. Kuntner, T. A. Blackledge; 32cr Wikipedia/M. Gallias; 32bl NASA, U.S.; 34c Naturepl; 35br FLPA; 39bl FLPA; 44–45 FLPA; 47tr Naturepl; 48c FLPA; 48bl FLPA; 52–53 Naturepl; 52bl Naturepl; 54tr FLPA; 56bl Robert Tyrrell; 59tc Centers for Disease Control and Prevention, U.S.; 59bc Centers for Disease Control and Prevention, U.S.; 60c Wikipedia/Miklos Schiberna; 61t Naturepl; 61br FLPA; 67tl FLPA; 67tr FLPA; 69br G. L. Banes; 74tr Naturepl; 83tr FLPA; 84–85 FLPA; 87tl Wikipedia/Pharaoh han; 90bl PRI-Kyoto/S. Carvalho; 98bl FLPA; 98br Naturepl; 102r Naturepl; 106bl FLPA; 110–111 Naturepl; 112cl Naturepl; 116bl Naturepl; 118tr Naturepl; 123tl Wikipedia/Llull, Tim Vickers; 125bl Centers for Disease Control and Prevention, U.S./Dr. Lyle Conrad; 128tl U.S. Navy/Brien Aho; 134–135 FLPA; 135br Dr. Fred Rumsey; 138tr Wikipedia/Ballista; 139tr Wikipedia/arenddehaas; 139bc Joel Garlich-Miller, U.S. FWS, U.S.; 139br Wikipedia/ E. J. Keller; 142–143 Dr. Paul Butler; 142bl Naturepl; 142br Dr. Martin Sayer/NERC Facility for Scientific Diving; 144r Mike Baird; 145br Wikipedia/Emgaol; 147tr Wikipedia/J. R. Bouldin; 148bl Wikipedia/Mason Brock; 149tl Ross D. E. MacPhee, American Museum of Natural History, New York, U.S.; 149cl Wikipedia/Klokeid; 149bl Natalie Tapson; 149bc Prof. Dr. Russell H. Vreeland/Prof. Dr. William Rosenzweig; 152tl NASA, U.S.; 152bl Joseph P. Vacanti Laboratory; 152br Prof. Dr. Stefano Piraino, Ph.D.; 153r Paramount/The Kobal Collection; 154tl Wikipedia/Alan Rockefeller; 154c Wikipedia/Peter17